Management Letters

In the Proven Pursuit of Excellence

New Edition

With his Telescope - The Right Way

ALAN SHARE

BE THE BEST YOU CAN BE

Equal Only Sometimes

Unequal Most Times

Always Different

PURSUE EXCELLENCE

Ordering Information:

Prime Seven Media
518 Landmann St.
Tomah City, WI 54660

Printed in the United States of America

WELCOME

I have had the pleasure of seeing the benefit of good management at close quarters for nearly half of a century. It has been one of the reasons why a company that I joined nearly fifty years ago has grown to one with a hundred branches nationwide and a multi-million £ turnover way, way beyond my expectations when I joined it as a clerk, trained by Alan Share's mother, Esther.

Subsequently I became PA to Alan, his successor Mike Browne, and his successor David Knight. They were all cut from the same timber. The pursuit of excellence. Being quick on your feet, reacting to a fast-changing world. Mutual respect stemming from what was initially a century old family company. Alan wrote these letters as his parting gift to his managers just a few years before he retired at the age of 60 with the company then a major player in retail furnishing in NE England. Subsequently, he had no financial interest in the company. But he never lost his love of it.

Whilst these letters were to benefit those who were managing the sale of upholstered furniture, their value relates to anyone managing the sale of widgets or making them for that matter. And they go even further than that, to anyone managing people.

We had an adage. Retail is detail. Everything is detail. Another adage. People buy people. I am sure that that is true in life generally. One of the topics in these letters is Kaizen, continuous improvement. Never stop learning. I personally witnessed that the university of life is the best teaching experience.

With Alan's management letters, true to his name, he now shares them with future generations. I can personally vouch for their benefit.

I hope that you will enjoy reading them. Lesley Sheraton

Assistant company secretary, SCS plc.

CONTENTS

INTRODUCTION

Chairman's Letter

It probably looks a bit strange to produce the INTRODUCTION at the conclusion, but it is much easier to decide what to say by way of introduction with 50 letters completed!

These letters have to do with management "know-how" - for "know-what" look elsewhere! They are about intuitive reactions to situations. Ultimately, management becomes as much this as almost anything else. Every manager has to develop for himself these intuitions and automatic responses, ridding himself of anything that fights them.

How would I describe the under-developed manager?

There's the "banana skin" manager who believes that because he has been promoted to manager, usually on the strength of some non-managerial skill, he knows all there is to know about managing people. Truth be told, you never fully know. There are always surprises. There is a lot to learn.

There's the "one-eyed ostrich" manager who accepts the credit when things go right but looks to blame everyone else when things go wrong and accordingly, never learns.

There's the "Teflon" manager where no words of guidance seem to stick.

There's the "back-to-front" manager, who thinks that yesterday's ways are more meaningful than tomorrow's opportunities.

And how would I describe the manager with antennae in working order?

A "ten foot tall" manager. and still growing.

A "power-steered" manager who makes it look so easy. A "razor sharp" manager. who has a cutting edge.

A manager with "three eyes - one eye capable of looking round the next corner - "two relatively large ears and one relatively small mouth!"

A "marathon" manager - who doesn't see managing as one short sprint after another, but as a long distance run you need to train for.

A manager, "well-fed and with a waggy tail", enjoying life generally. And a manager who can look himself in the eye in the mirror every morning and again in the evening.

He does not think he has ever reached his destination, for if he had he would have nowhere else to go!

These letters are written for him, to read, inwardly digest, then dip into from time to time.

TEMPO

As you know, I quite like using my word-processor - no typex, no rubber, and no wastepaper basket.

It occurred to me that I could put to paper each week a comment, a thought, and maybe even a criticism of how we go about things which would be of value. Fifteen minutes from me here, and fifteen minutes from you after you have read it - in the car or in the bath - thinking about it.

So, what is to be my first "thought for the week"?

TEMPO - a word I first came to understand on the chess board.

When you think of that game, you realise that it does not mean speed! Chess is a war-game, and "Tempo" is a war-word even when you are playing the game with a good friend.

What it means is grabbing the initiative and holding it. Chess is never neutral - except when it reaches stalemate, a draw.

White or black has the initiative, the tempo - dictating the course of the game.

In music, one note seems to command the next, the same idea. It is a form of aggression - controlled, concealed, and quite deliberate. When you understand it, you then have to learn the technique to go for it. It very quickly becomes an instinctive way of doing things.

What has all this to do with management in this company? When a manufacturer doesn't deliver when he should, when a customer doesn't pay or doesn't accept delivery, they have the "tempo" and you have lost it.

So how do you get the "tempo" and how do you keep it?

The answer is very very simple. You focus on what you want from the outset. You get agreed lead-times in writing via a signed service level agreement from the manufacturer, which includes a penalty clause payment, should they let you and the customer down on delivery.

So, question: how do you win the "tempo" with your own staff and with head office, too?

Remember you can't be one step ahead, if you don't think one step ahead, and remember, you don't win by being the nice guy, but if you give that appearance, you get the best of all worlds. That's when art, or is it artfulness, goes alongside technique.

Remember business is dynamic not static. It is an engine that needs to be driven. You are the driver.

KISS

Last week I wrote about TEMPO and about the importance of seizing the initiative and holding it, so that you control events and events do not control you.

The one place where this should always happen is inside your own branch.

When that is the case, you can feel it in the air. Eyes smile naturally. The mood is relaxed yet purposeful. If people are walking about they are going somewhere. If they are talking, they are not just chatting. The eyes actually say it all! And the smile is probably the most important of all.

I have the feeling that more important than any words spoken to a customer coming into the store, is a welcoming smile.

Here are a few "smiling" exercises for you.

1. When you get up and stand in front of the mirror. You may not feel like smiling at this time of the day but try. Try first smiling with your mouth alone. It's physically impossible. Now, smile with your eyes, and your whole face lights up. Actually, your whole being lights up. Your voice changes. Your mood lights up.

2. Next, when you are in a traffic jam, smile at the driver in the car next to you. He will smile back. Even in adversity smiling is infectious.
3. When you are dealing with a difficult situation on the telephone smile as you speak - believe it or not I have just had to practice what I am preaching! It didn't solve anything, but it made me feel better.
4. Try smiling to yourself, but make sure no-one is looking as they may think you're going round the bend.

I shall write more about feelings as against thoughts, but KISS "Keep It Simple Stupid" must be the essence of these letters.

So, remember the old song "When you're smiling, when you're smiling the whole world smiles with you." Here is my own personal smile-o-meter.

0 -2 smiles a day - "let me get out of here quick".
3 - 10 smiles a day - "life's a serious business"
11 - 20 smiles a day - "and, a bit of fun, too."
over 20 smiles a day - "let's share it."

COMMUNICATION

My topic this week is COMMUNICATION.

There is a famous playwriter who has made a fortune for himself writing plays showing how two people can be in the same room apparently talking to each other, but as neither is listening to the other, all you get is Gobbledygook. The conversation is about as meaningful as that between two people who are stone deaf.

Many people think they can talk, but they don't listen. They don't "tune in" to the other person's needs and requirements, and don't therefore ask the right questions.

If you do want to communicate you do have to listen, you do have to look as well - body language talks too - and you do have to ask questions.

You also must know whether you are expressing thoughts or feelings and listening to thoughts or feelings. If you don't, it is like being on a different waveband.

If you are in a school classroom, you expect to use your brain first and think. Of course, if you feel for the subject your brain may work better.

If you are in a furniture showroom, you will feel first. Is it warm and Welcoming? Are the colours bright and cheerful? Do you feel -no, not think - you can trust the people you are dealing with? Feelings start with first impressions. And if your feelings are favourable, you will then use your brain more purposefully. Will the suite you like fit your room? How will you pay for it? I am sure that when people make a buying decision their feelings come before their thoughts. Richard Denny says emotions have been calculated at 84% of a buying decision!

Hence, the welcoming smile, the well laid out store, the music, and all the things that - to quote a famous London store that does just this - "nourish and tantalise" the senses - and getting rid of all those things that can irritate them.

So here are two exercises:

1. List the plusses and minuses that lead to good feelings or bad feelings about your store, the display, the pricing, and approach of your staff. These are your thoughts and feelings but walk into your store and see yourself as the customer!
2. Ask your sales staff how much talking and how much listening they do when they are selling. I have heard the adage that we were born with one mouth and two ears and should use them in ratio. Do you agree? And do we?

TRAINING

Every now and again I hear a manager greeting a potential customer with those well-worn words "Can I help you" or "Is there something you are looking for?"

I did believe that that form of welcome was just about the weakest in the game.

As I understand it, questions starting "Who", "What", "Where" and "When" demand an answer, but the answer just cannot be "No, thank you" or "I'm just looking", unless they are deaf!

So, what am I to make of a situation where a manager of all people who is supposed to have made his way in the trade by selling makes such an elementary error? In this world, people tend to see and copy what others do.

I guess the point I am really trying to make here, is that the manager has to set the standard himself and ask for performance, measured against that standard. Tempo!! Smile!!

Put it another way. My topic for this week is TRAINING.

Have you come across the phrase "learning curve"? All too often it is the curve of forgetfulness! One day after a factory visit, or a training session you have forgotten part of what you learnt, two days after you have forgotten a little more, and so on. After a month, you may as well not have gone in the first place!

So, what is the answer?

The professional will get his instinctive response right every time. Like riding a bicycle. You don't forget. The professional will evolve a technique, honed by day-to-day experience. The professional will know that he never, ever stops learning. Learning - the best learning - is not once or twice a year, but every day and every moment of every day. It is on the job! That way the learning curve goes upwards not downwards. There is only one source for this on-the-job training and that is the manager. Identifying and correcting weaknesses, praising and "reinforcing" strengths, especially that.

You can only do that if you look, listen and act, or should I say react. and, set an example!

Question - do you?

I shall enjoy reading your report on training. I am sure that you will not be waiting until January to implement it!

MURPHY

Has anyone seen Murphy recently?

It would be just like him to pop up now and spoil somebody's Xmas and New Year, too, if he can manage it!

Last I saw of him was when he was lurking behind our computer. He loves our computer. It is his second home. His first - well, that's in our service department.

This isn't a comment on John Bainbridge, Bernadette, or Pam and those working alongside them. It is a comment on the worlds they inhabit. There are just so many wonderful opportunities for Murphy to get in there and have a good time.'

Is there a way of dealing with him? First, you have got to understand how his mind works, and secondly where he likes to operate.

He always wants to add to a problem that is already there. Ideally, he would like to make it insoluble and to cost a lot of money into the bargain. If he can cause a scandal in the press, he gets a special prize. If he can arrive when you least expect it, he gets special pleasure.

He will mislay messages, run off with keys, not to mention vans, he will mix up stock tickets, and he quite likes setting the burglar alarm off. He will bounce cheques to coincide with urgent deliveries. If there is a choice of two spare parts, he will make sure that the wrong one is sent, and if a choice of three, he will make sure that the second one is wrong too. He has been known to send the wrong one twice!

There is really only one way to deal with him. If you expect him, you can actually head him off altogether. He rarely goes where he is expected.

So, my advice is look for the troublesome situations, and assume that everything is wrong until you have yourself proved that it is right. Don't take anyone else's word for it, unless confirmed in writing.

Challenge: £1 from me to the first person spotting Murphy and showing him the door. A clue, he was last seen in one of our warehouses tampering with one of our suites and with a pile of stock tickets in his jacket pocket.

PACE

I have written about "Tempo". Today, I am writing about "PACE".

"Pace" isn't necessarily "Speed". You can, after all, have a slow pace. It is controlled speed.

You hear the word used of the professional footballer who "paces" 90 minutes so that he won't run out of energy in the last ten minutes. You will hear the word used of the long-distance runner who still wants the energy to "kick" for the last hundred metres.

It is a form of personal energy conservation, so that when you really want to move you have the reserves to do so.

If you pace what you are doing, you can put your foot down on your personal accelerator any time you like and get results.

Why do I choose the subject now?

Well, January Sale time is the time when you have to draw on your reserves, get the adrenalin going, and keep it going. Remember, enthusiasm is infectious, the speed you walk contagious, the salesperson's first sale of the day to be praised, and the last sale of the day - (the better it is. The later it is, Look for the best in everything - the biggest sale, the suite you most wanted out, leather targets, bedding targets, personal targets.

If you are pleased show that you are, if you are not pleased, best keep it to yourself - for the time being!

Those who know about these things describe this as "positive reinforcement". I think it is just a matter of showing what you feel.

It is, however, amazing how easy it is to say, "well done", and show appreciation and yet how often thanks and appreciation are not expressed, and effort taken for granted.

And, when it comes to our customers, make them feel especially welcome, make them feel that it is bargain time, that the reductions are real and that they can, if they are quick, get a great buy.

The message is Sell - Sell - Sell, but make sure that everyone enjoys it, both the buyer and the seller.

TEMPO! PACE! SMILE! MERRY XMAS AND A VERY HAPPY, HEALTHY AND PROSPEROUS NEW YEAR!

PUT IT IN WRITING

I often say, "put it in writing" or, if it is an inquest, ask "did you put it in writing?"

As you may or may not know, although Mike and I are very much on speaking terms and occupy adjoining offices, even we write to each other.

It is worth thinking this one through.

What does writing achieve?

1. It sorts your own mind out, and that's not unimportant.
2. It brings a subject to the top of the pile.
3. If it contains a recommendation, as it should, it is the first step towards action.
4. It isn't so easily lost sight of. The stray thought in a conversation can so easily be forgotten and not acted upon.
5. It puts the matter on the record, especially if you keep a copy and put it in your pending file. I hope you have a pending file. Ask Lesley about this if you haven't.
6. And, it will go on your record if you have got it right -and you yourself can make sure of that.

The story is told of the chap who confessed to his wife that he owed his neighbour Harry £500, and he couldn't pay him.

"You don't look very worried about it." said his wife. "No, I've just told Harry, and he's the one that's worried!"

That's another benefit from writing.

There is, of course, a right and a wrong way to write.

If it is not on one side of a sheet of paper, it is probably too long. It should argue to a conclusion or a recommendation. And, if you think back to my first letter on "Tempo" it will be so worded to demand an answer by a date. Of course, it won't actually demand, it might suggest or be grateful for, but if it is properly worded, it won't get forgotten, will it?

Question: what gripe have you got that would be much better unloaded on someone else, so he can have the gripe instead? I suppose it may end up in a piece of writing between Mike and myself!

DESIGN

There are two subjects that should be compulsory for all managers - one is Design and the other is Psychology.

One determines how things work and the other how people work! Quite a few of my letters have been about Psychology - just say people. The topic for this letter is DESIGN.

I had no training in design appreciation. Art at school, so far as I was concerned, was about drawing and painting and bad drawing and painting at that. Just a few in the class had real talent.

In work and travel, I began to see what I had missed. The first lesson came from a graphic artist showing how choice of typeface, colour, paper, shape and proportion could improve the message and make it readable. World famous paintings in Art Galleries and Exhibitions showed the effect of colour, line, texture and light on mood and effect.

Visits to Denmark, Switzerland, Italy and France showed flair in interior design and fashion, interior design in public buildings as well as private homes.

We are not very good in this country. Go round the inside of the Civic Centre in Sunderland, designed by a top British Architect Sir Basil Spence for a totally boring experience!

Design has been a kind of elitist concept, with good UK designers tempted to work abroad, because they had no recognition at home.

We need to feel comfortable with Design, because our work is intimately connected with Design. This enables you to communicate with those who create design - furniture manufacturers, John Branskey, admen, - and those who increasingly want to buy it - our customers!

Colour, its relationship to mood and effect, lighting likewise, texture and feel, scale and proportion, line and balance, feminine and masculine mood, decorative effects, materials - their features and their benefits &c.

There is no simple route into this world, but using your eyes intelligently helps. Look at the Sony Walkman, German fashion, Glossy magazines, the London Tube map, travelling irons, and try dipping into an illustrated book of some of the world's greatest painters Van Goch, Monet, Lowry.

This is all to do with feelings, and instincts, with mood and with pleasure.

It is a worthwhile project for 1991.

MOTIVATION

"I am 100% committed." Many people in the company would say this, but all that that means is that they think they are giving of their utmost. I believe that everyone has unrealised potential.

Karate shows you how to liberate incredible latent physical power. This letter focusses on MOTIVATION as one of the ways to liberate the human dynamic, combat complacency, and provide enormous additional job satisfaction and personal fulfilment and enormous benefit to the company and to colleagues, too. If one person is going to be motivated, another person must be the motivator! YOU!

The first time I saw this was when I visited our advertising guru in Broken Arrow, Tulsa Oklahoma! Bob Keiningham told me that he got much more satisfaction himself getting the best of a salesforce than advertising yet another Gigantic Storewide Sale. A training lesson offered the possibility of long-term gain, an advert short term gain at best.

Bob made the point to me that everyone should be encouraged to identify a goal, a personal objective, something to work for. Everyone is different, so the goals are all different. What you have to do is to get people to identify their goals, to cost them, and then to show people precisely how to attain them.

The fact that everyone does want to improve the material quality of their own and their family's lives in the next 12 months is no.1 motivating force because it is continuing and ever present. You, as the motivator, have to help to make that aspiration attainable.

The next "motivating" force. Everyone enjoys winning, though they don't always own up to it! In this case, it's not the size of the prize, but the fact of a prize and the recognition that goes with it. Correspondingly, no-one likes losing as you don't like to live with the badge of failure constantly visible. So, If there are going to be competitions, you must keep them short and snappy!

The third motivating force is relaxation! That, I believe, is the secret of Karate. You can try too hard. If life is too tense, effort and stress are totally counterproductive. It has to be possible to breathe enjoyment into a job, constantly looking for new and rewarding aspects of it, and finding praise for a job well done. You have a big role here.

The fourth motivating force is the infectious optimism, enthusiasm, and get-up-and-go spirit that you yourself generate all the time, especially first thing in the morning, especially last thing at night! Exercise: Consider your team under these three heads - Commitment, Performance, and Potential, e.g., 100:60:80 or 80:60:65 or 50:50:50! The message: Commitment leads to growth.

DECISION TAKING

A couple of Weeks ago, waiting for an overdue train at King's Cross on a cold January evening, with the cold marble floor chilling my feet and legs right up to my knees, I found myself in a very interesting conversation with a man in charge of the Crown Prosecution Service!

I forget what provoked him to quote Lord Denning, that very famous judge, but he said that Lord Denning had once remarked "Be right . . . or be wrong, but do not be in doubt."

That must be good advice for a judge to give himself. His job is to make decisions and not to agonise about them afterwards. Is it also good advice for a manager? It is worth a little thought in a quiet moment.

The subject of this letter is DECISION TAKING.

There is no doubt that indecision and indecisiveness are enemies. Managers are paid to take decisions, and sometimes a bad decision will be better than no decision at all.

Some good decisions are hard decisions to make. General's decisions cost lives. Our decisions may cost jobs, or less painfully money. Some good decisions take time to think through and work through.

Some bad decisions are easy. Not to make a decision "just yet" is itself a decision! Some bad decisions are "short termist", ignoring long term consequences - this is one of the great weaknesses of UK Ltd. where the large companies have to announce their results to the Stock Market every six months! They often don't take the long view. Going for a "quick buck" is always going to be a temptation.

Some people don't take decisions because they don't want to put their heads above the parapet, some because they file the difficult problems in their "Manyana" file and some because they don't see the problem in the first place. The problem you don't see you don't have the additional problem of dealing with! I don't sense that there is a lot of that in this company, but it is worth posing the question of whether there is any.

Question: are you postponing a decision not because it is a wise decision to postpone it, but because it is a cosy one?

Don't use this to justify the bad decision, hastily reached with insufficient information, but I suspect that not just in Courts of Law, or in management but in life generally, Lord Denning is right!

FILING

Lesley keeps my company paperwork with the outside World in very good order. I want to make this clear at the outset. She invariably can put her hand on any letter or address in her files, and once a month she puts my Pending File on my desk as a firm and gentle reminder to me not to postpone my decision taking and to remind others to do likewise.

I do, however, have other paperwork, and if you come into my office, you see some of it piled on my desk. Some of it also gets pushed in haste into filing drawers.

Yes, despite what I said in my last letter about decision taking, I plead guilty to not taking some decisions myself! The "too difficult to deal with today" matters, the "this can wait until tomorrow" letters, and the "this really should go into the wastepaper basket" junk mail all pile up with weekly reports and analysis sheets.

I sometimes think that it creates the illusion that I am busier than I am. I know it creates the belief that I am less organised, at least always than I believe that I am.

Why am I parading all this?

Well, I have just sorted myself out. It is amazing how much paper is totally dead anyway, and the start of a New Year is as good a time as any to get rid of it.

It does, however, help to file paperwork away tidily, and FILING is today's theme.

There is no doubt that "Filing" is good for you! I was able to put into practice that training tip that you should always do the most difficult and unpleasant job first, so that everything afterwards becomes progressively easier.

Then, you must sort your thoughts before you sort your papers! Deciding what goes where is a very good mental discipline.

-memos, minutes, reports, correspondence - alive or dead, and soon.

The reward of being able to put your hand immediately on what you want is enormous.

What I can't understand is why the last few pieces of paper stubbornly refuse to be pigeonholed. I know, however, what it means. Unless I am careful, in three months' time I will have to start all over again!

A thought: Our printer really has got diarrhea.
An exercise: are you in charge of your paperwork?
A question: do you file these letters sequentially in a separate file?

NEEDS AND WANTS

I believe that there has been some discussion on whether our sales staff find out what our customers' needs are. This is obviously a very important aspect of professional selling. This week I would like to pose a question that is relevant to that discussion. If you are talking about NEEDS are you also talking about WANTS, and if you are, are you talking about the same thing? If they are different, how important is the difference?

A person needs a car, he wants a Porsche he probably doesn't need a Porsche! A person needs a meal, he wants Caviar, he certainly does not need Caviar! Put this way, it is quite important to the car salesman and the restauranteur to distinguish between needs and wants.

It must also be for us - not just in selling, but in advertising as well.

Needs tend to be basic and rational. Getting married, moving into a new home . . . need a new suite. Square room......... need a settee and two chairs, a rectangular room.........need a 3seater. and a 2-seater. Moving into sheltered housing,... ......a small suite.

Wants tend to be aspirational, acquisitive, emotional. You actually may not need at all something you want. A fashion garment is a good illustration of that. A leather suite, a print suite are very often "wants" not "needs", so is the comfort of a high back suite.

Needs are general, wants can be specific. A bargain is usually a want!

I have the feeling that if a person sees a suite that seems to meet a need, he will look further to see if he can find another that meets it better. If he sees a suite he wants . . . he will buy it! We're back to distinguishing between thoughts and feelings and to recognising the emotional side of buying and selling that I wrote about in letter no.3. We're also into detective work. A little bit of Sherlock Holmes stuff won't go amiss. The car people drive up in will tell you something of their aspirations. The family they arrive with will tell you something of their needs, such as their age, also whether their hands have been scratched by their cat!

So, the exercise this week:

1. Identify five questions that go to determine a customer's needs and five that go to determine his wants.
2. If you are quizzing a salesperson as to what he has found out about his customers, just see whether he knows their wants as well as their needs!

MEETINGS

We spend a huge chunk of our lives in bed. So the bed manufacturers remind us. We spend another huge chunk of our lives attending meetings. I recently saw a John Cleese Video training film entitled MEETINGS, BLOODY MEETINGS. That is my topic for this week.

Whether you are convening a meeting or attending one, you must think it through in advance, ie. you must plan it.

The first part of planning is determining the AGENDA - "agenda" is a Latin word that means "Things that must be done"! It is critical to remember that. Not "Things that must be talked about"! You have to address the matter logically. First, what did we agree last time we met that had to be done? MINUTES. Do we have an accurate record? What have we done/not done that we agreed to do? MATTERS ARISING unless they are otherwise on the Agenda. What do other people want us to think about? CORRESPONDENCE. What new facts do we have to take account of-usually financial! FINANCE.

Now list ITEMS FOR DISCUSSION in a logical order. Where information is available to assist discussion, ensure that that information is in writing and attached to the Agenda. Ideally all of this should be in people's hands 7 days before the meeting and certainly 48 hours. Papers circulated at a meeting do not allow for proper thought.

Don't think that the only person with the responsibility for tabling documentation is the person convening the meeting. Ever one should consider giving advance notice of his or her contribution ideally with precise recommendations for action.

Remember - I hope you do - my first letter on TEMPO. This is very important when it comes to meetings. So, read it again here.

If you are convening the meeting, think of the people invited and the contribution you expect them to make. Be fair, give them advance notice. Think of the people not invited. Should they be invited? Should they be informed before or after the event? If you are attending a meeting, again think of the others who are going and think through the implications.

ANY OTHER BUSINESS in case you have missed something important.

DATE OF NEXTMEETINGS. Don't leave a meeting without planning the next one or even the next two or three whilst everyone is there. That is the best way to progress decisions made. MINUTES. These should be brief and to the point, setting out those present, what was noted for the record and what was agreed for action, the initials of the person to take action entered down the right-hand side as a memo to that person and to facilitate monitoring. AGREED? AGREED!

SERVICE

My topic this week is SERVICE.

This is a strange word. We are in what is often described as the "Service Sector", but the word service does seem to carry undertones of sub-servience, and quite often people seem to deny themselves the satisfactions that come from serving a customer well on that account.

I suspect that even the caring professions sometimes fall into the same trap.

Now, "I am your humble and obedient servant" has quite rightly disappeared. But what has replaced it? "Assuring you of my best attention at all times." Rhubarb, rhubarb stuff! Words carrying little or no sincerity, even though they are immediately followed by "yours sincerely"!

Let's look at one or two other countries to see whether we can understand the word service better.

Japan - on our study tour last year, I learnt that shop assistants spent their first six weeks (no, not six minutes) learning how to bow. I personally much prefer the warmth of the western handshake, which is as alien to the Japanese as the bow is to us.

It is, however, worth thinking about that bow. It points to who we are actually dependent on! Our customers! And it shows them respect. Respect is a key aspect of service. It is important to recognise it.

Switzerland - breakfasting once in a small hotel in the village of Grindlewald, I was suddenly conscious of the waitress absolutely noiselessly removing the plates and cutlery from the place next to mine. The other things I remember about all the waitresses were their attractive Swiss attire, their welcoming smiles, and the fact that they were multi-lingual! Professional service carried with it real skill and knowledge and a care for fine detail.

Rotary - the international "Service Club" I belong to - proclaims "Service before self", and that is another aspect of the word. You have to be unselfish of your time to give that extra something that can often make all the difference.

You can take a real pride in being of service to someone. You can get real satisfaction, too. Those letters of thanks that we post up are truly testimonials for those who receive them.

Exercise: review the letters in your showcase. Who is prompting them......and who needs a gentle reminder about real service?

Remember, here, we are not just talking about sales staff. We are very definitely including everyone in the team.

"Yours sincerely"

MONEY/CASHFLOW

This week my topic is MONEY, or more precisely CASH FLOW. What has provoked me to think about it is the perusal of our accounts for our last financial year in connection with the company's annual general meeting.

We believe that profit is important, and it is. Cash flow, in its own way, can be even more important. Companies that have over-borrowed or who allow their customers to hold on to money they owe can get into difficulties even though they are in profit.

It is amazing where the money goes - an extra £350k on our stock - some of this money spent on the stock in Middlesbrough South Bank, some on higher cost merchandise such as leather, our repair bills up £130k because of the work at Villiers Street, the cost of fitting out South Bank and constructing new warehousing in Stockton, the loss at "The Other Room" over £40k paid off our long-term borrowing, and corporation tax. Despite all of this, last year the amount of interest we paid on our long-term borrowing was matched by the interest we received on current cash balances at the Bank, and this was not at the price of keeping our own suppliers waiting for payment, so we were able to secure very substantial settlement discounts and the good service that good payers can demand.

So, my letter this week is to thank you for helping to achieve all that, for helping to get the money in!

At the beginning of October last year, we had £350k in customer prepayments. Depreciation - writing off previous capital purchases -amounted to over £150k. Add to that our notional rents and trading profit and we ended up in a very healthy situation in which to face this tough year for trading. This year, with interest rates likely to remain high - I think that we can expect only limited reductions - cash flow is again going to be very important to us.

The rules of the game are very, very simple.

1. Large deposits when orders are taken - full payment if possible.
2. Full payment when furniture is available for delivery.
3. High rate of stockturn, with good stock management. Cash in the bank is much better than "dead" stock.
4. And, husbanding our resources together with profitable trading.

This is a game everyone can play.

MANAGERS MANUAL

I have been writing these letters now for about four months. This letter is designed to check out first what you make of them, secondly what you do with them, and thirdly what topics you would like future letters to deal with.

I hope that you are keeping these letters filed consecutively. I also hope that from time to time you glance through back issues. They do not run in any logical sequence, but together they become a kind of MANAGER'S MANUAL.

You need to have instinctive reactions to situations. What those instinctive reactions should be is primarily what these letters are about. Seeing/listening/asking - thinking - acting.

You have a responsibility for training all your staff - getting them to get the best from themselves - and some of these letters should be helping in that direction, too.

These Letters also convey information, some of which you may already have, but expressed in the wider context of good management, not just in the context of the management of your own branch. You have to see the "whole" as well as the "part".

Do they have any other value so far as you are concerned? And do you use them? If so, how and when? Do you discuss them with your Sales Manager? Do you discuss them with your sales or office staff. Do you put anything in writing to them? Management is about being proactive, not just reactive. Lastly, what new topics would you like me to cover. Steve provoked me to write about "NEEDS and WANTS". My thoughts for future topics

> - I am not asking for suggestions because I am drying up – include STRESS - OUR CUSTOMERS', CURTAINS, COLOUR IN OUR LIVES, and REWARDS AND SATISFACTIONS. I would welcome some ideas from you.

Maybe the next but one letter will be the best response! Give yourself a few days to work it out.

STRESS

I was recently party to the choice of a designer to be charged with the task of designing a new voluntary Code of Practice for the Furniture and Carpet Industry, new helpful labelling information - like road signs in the Highway Code, and a Logo for shop-doors and company advertising clearly identifying those retailers and manufacturers that traded in a responsible fashion.

One of the designers, in fact the successful one, seemed to read the situation he had to deal with more clearly than anyone else. Amongst other things he pointed out to us was the state of mind of the average shopper for furniture.

STRESS is very much a buzz word today. People tend to talk of STRESS MANAGEMENT in relation to staff. He talked about it in relation to our customers!

The first thing that needs to be said is that STRESS is not all bad! Some people work better stressed, when the adrenalin is flowing.

On the other hand, our positioning statement is RELAX and that is the exact opposite and for very good reason.

The worst thing about STRESS is that it can paralyse the brain and kill off any good feelings that may be around.

So, what is STRESS? It is mainly worry. Some worries are real. Some are imaginary. Many are exaggerated. "Some of the griefs you have cured and the sharpest you have survived, but what torments of pain you endured ... from evils that never arrived." Someone else's words not mine!

What are shoppers worried about? That they are going to make the wrong decision that they are going to spend more than they should that they are going to make the wrong decision, that the salesperson is a conman that they are going to make the wrong decision.

Don't assume that the first sight the shopper has of you or your sales staff will automatically dispel all this! The stressed shopper walks around in a suit of armour to protect himself. You have to persuade him to take it off.

The warm smiling welcome and all the reassurances he receives that, at least in SCS, his anxieties are groundless will all work towards that state of relaxation where he will, as he should, positively enjoy spending his money and will be able to spot the right buying decision and make it. To offer that 6 days a week, nine or more hours a day, is the challenge that you personally have.

Here is a test for you. Look at your customers 5 minutes after they have visited your branch. Are they beginning to RELAX or are they still STRESSED? Incidentally, if you and your staff are stressed because there's nothing on the pad, you have to be very professional to make sure it doesn't show! It is very contagious

CONFIDENCE

Thank you, Barry! At least one Manager was quick off the mark with a short and professional reply to Letter No. 16. You suggested three topics - morale boosting, dealing with pressure, and confidence building. I shall take the last first. I was thinking of writing about CONFIDENCE and your letter has provoked me to work through with you some aspects of this.

What is CONFIDENCE about anyway? It has to do with knowledge, with patience and with self-esteem.

Let's look at these three in sequence.

Knowledge first. Very few, if any, believe they know it all. Quite a lot of people believe that they know enough. That is the greatest trap a manager or anyone in authority can fall into. Margaret Thatcher thought she knew enough about the Poll Tax. Nigel Lawson about Exchange Rates. The Lord Chief Justice about the guilt of the Birmingham 6. Marietta Higgs about child abuse in Cleveland.

These people thought that they would not have got where they were if they didn't know these things. They then used their authority to get their way. They then fell flat on their face!

In all walks of life, I find myself having to confront the complacency and, at times, the conceit of people who smugly believe that they know. It is especially so with the legal and medical professions.

And, what happens when things go wrong? It is all the other man's mistake. You remember, I am sure, the Richard Denny tape. One finger points accusingly at someone else. Where do the other three point?

It is important to believe that you never ever know enough. You never ever stop learning. Recognising that does not make you less confident. It makes you better at your job, and that makes you more confident. Success reinforces success.

Next, experience. This is obviously relevant to self-confidence, but with a big proviso and that is that you are prepared to learn from it! You have to look at those three fingers when things go wrong. If you don't, you are not just stupid, you look stupid! There's no praise in that, and praise reinforces confidence.

Lastly, self-esteem. You have actually got to like yourself. That is why a good and healthy diet, fresh air and exercise, and smart dress have a real relevance. You look how you feel. So, feel great!

TECHNIQUE ON MORALE BOOSTING

Last week, I wrote about confidence. This week, I shall take Barry's other suggested theme "TECHNIQUES ON MORALE BOOSTING." It is worth turning back to Letters No.1. on Tempo, No.9 on Motivation, and No.18 on Confidence. All of these are relevant and make the clear point that the onus is on the Manager here, your own self-confidence being a very key element.

Can I begin with a few axioms that you might find useful:

1. Any team, working as a team, will be much more productive than the individuals in a team working separately.
2. If the manager doesn't set standards and ask for performance, there is absolutely no-one else around to do so.
3. Staff left to their own endeavours will probably deliver no more than half of their full potential. Competent management should lift this by up to 20%, inspiring management by up to 30%. (The claim "I'm giving 100%" is meaningless!) They will thank you for the improvement. It Is more money in their pocket and more job satisfaction.
4. The learning curve (the curve of forgetfulness) is downwards for off the job training. The learning

curve (the curve of real learning) is upwards in relation to on-the-job training.

5. If people switch on when praised and switch off when criticised, you have to develop your own technique for correcting faults.

If that is the background to personnel management, how do you plan to motivate your staff? You will then have no problem with morale. Remember what "motivate" means. It means to "make move". It means more than that. It means that they should move at the pace you set and in the direction you point to and not at the pace they set and in the direction they choose. I actually believe that people like and respond to firm, clear and decisive leadership. So, give it!

What we are talking about is delegating jobs and then checking out whether they have been done properly. We are talking about agreeing targets - it's no good setting them if they are not agreed - and then monitoring whether they are being achieved. We are talking about you declaring your needs from your staff in terms of their appearance and their performance and asking them to declare their needs from you, in relation to matters such as training or whatever.

All of this does not happen of its own accord. It must be planned to happen. Otherwise, it starts and then ends up in the wastepaper basket of good intentions.

Exercise: Go back to Letter No. 13 and plan your regular staff meetings according to the guidelines set out there and with the objectives set out here. Send me your agenda!

HOW TO RIDE
THE TIGER

George poses the question as to how to overcome objections and threats. Barry poses the question as to how to deal with pressure. So, the theme of this letter is HOW TO RIDE THE TIGER!

If you understand that it is a tiger and not a rocking-horse you are part of the way to dealing with the situation!

I can never understand how anyone should want to climb Mount Everest. Tunstall Hill is enough for me. I can never understand how anyone should want to be a deep-sea diver. I like to have my feet on the bottom and my head above the water at all times! Some people cannot understand why anyone should want to be in retailing - the uncertainty, the competition, the consumerists, the bank manager!

There is really only one answer to objections, threats and pressure.

ENJOY THEM!

It may be easy for me to say this, but I am afraid that if you feel that all you have to learn is how best to SUFFER them, you will get quite a mauling from that tiger!

For every threat, there is an opportunity. The Office of Fair Trading is threatening the Furniture Industry with its highly critical report on the product we sell and the way we sell it.

The Industry is using the situation to enhance the good and responsible side which does exist and then sell it.

For every objection, the professional will have an answer. The person who is unprofessional will not even hear the objection. And, as for pressure, the real entrepreneur will revel in the challenge of it.

I meet quite a few people in education. I must tell them that they have a wrong perception of retailing, if they think it is a safe, cosy dull, repetitive and unrewarding job. I must tell them that at times it is unsafe, uncomfortable, and unpredictable, but potentially it is very rewarding, and much to my very great surprise, I enjoy it.

Consider the situation that your sales staff must deal with every day. Making a sale. The threat is there alright. The customer will walk out without buying. The objections will be there as well. The suite will not look right. The price is too high. The pressure is there, too . . . to make the sale or feel sick!

With the threat comes the opportunity to sell. With the objection comes the benefits of buying. With the pressure comes the pleasure of making the sale, and the more you have made the sale on your terms rather than conceded and made the sale on your customers' terms the greater the satisfaction! Who said retailing was easy?

TECHNIQUE OF NEGOTIATION

Malcolm has suggested that I talk about "power of silence" as a tool to make someone give you information. This has obviously to be seen in a wider context, namely the TECHNIQUE OF NEGOTIATION.

I have picked up a few ideas from other people over the years and I put them down here not as definitive answers but as weapons for your armoury which you choose to use as and when you wish.

The first question that I pose is what sort of relationship is the salesperson trying to establish with his customer? At the outset he will certainly represent SCS. At the end of the day should he be representing the customer to SCS? Should he seem to be changing sides? It is worth thinking this through in relation to the way a sale is structured.

Whether he actually changes sides or not, he should be a friend and counsellor, a person to be trusted, a person who is fair and understanding. How do you get into that situation ... quickly? It is only when you have reached that point that silence in the conversation, a pause, may encourage the customer to volunteer information that you might not even have thought to ask for.

If you pause too soon, the customer may simply say "Thank you" and go!

My second question is who should suggest the price at which the deal is to be struck? I know that the temptation is certainly there for the salesperson to suggest a figure or a deal, putting it first to the customer and then if he agrees putting it to the manager for approval. However, the rule of negotiation I have come across is not that one.

Whether you are selling or buying to get the best deal for yourself, get the other party to name a figure first. The salesperson can then himself negotiate upwards indicating what he thinks the manager "might just agree to." If the salesperson goes in first with a figure and doesn't get the deal at that price, the only thing he can then do is to reduce his price still further.

So, what does this all amount to? First, establish trust and confidence. Then ask how much they would be willing to pay for the suite you sense they want, then pause and you may get the most important information of all, the beginnings of the making of a deal, and, of course, a natural close.

I used this technique myself when I bought my latest Volvo. I invited the salesperson to tell me how much he would offer in part-exchange. He asked me how much I was looking for and I refused to give him any idea at all. He gave me a figure which really wasn't very good. I rejected it but indicated that if he gave me an offer I could not refuse, I would not refuse. He did!

If you or your staff have any thoughts or experiences to share on this topic, let me know, and I will circulate them.

ENTREPRENEUR

Are you an ENTREPRENEUR?
Are you a successful ENTREPRENEUR?

Before you read further, write on a piece of paper whether you think you are and, if you think you are, what it actually means to be one.

I pose this question this week as I have posed it to myself in two different situations recently. In the Furniture Industry Action Group, I have sensed that it is at this point that members have divided. Some are entrepreneurial, some are not. Also, at a meeting with some friends in the educational field, I suggested that there were too many economists and accountants in high places who were not, by their training, entrepreneurial, and yet were in positions that required entrepreneurial flair. Did education deliver this? From the answers given, I don't think they understood the question!

So, what is it to be an entrepreneur?

My answer is that it is to "create profitable buying and selling situations". And to be a successful entrepreneur … to maximise that. It is not enough to "accept profitable buying and selling situations." And why are economists and accountants very often not entrepreneurial? Because their training is to analyse buying and selling situations, and not create them.

Does it necessarily involve taking risks? The answer must be yes. Starting a new venture, opening a new branch, placing an advertisement, all of these are entrepreneurial activities, and if you get them wrong you lose money, and if you get them badly wrong you go broke. But if you get them right, that is the bait. There is, however, a great difference between a gamble and a business speculation. The difference lies in the fact that in business the professional will evaluate and minimise the risk. He can never remove it altogether. That is why there are the rewards!

There are so many people around that do not want to take any risks at all. In many cases, they are so blinkered in their approach that they do not even see the opportunity to take a risk! That is why there is a huge opportunity, especially in this non-entrepreneurial country ("Entrepreneur" is a French derivative), for those who do.

Do you have to be ruthless? You do have to go for the ball. Changing the metaphor "If you see a competitor drowning, stick a hosepipe in his mouth" may be overstating it just a little! So, let's say "The successful entrepreneur won't muck about!" It's about having the guts as well as having the brains.

So, do you accept business, or do you create it? Do you book sales or do you "generate" them? Do you go along with trends, or do you try to buck them? Are you dictated to by events, or do you dictate to them?

What have you put down on your piece of paper? Do you need to amend it?

DECLARE YOUR NEEDS

This week, something which I believe is a lesson in living as well as a lesson in management. DECLARE YOUR NEEDS. That may sound so obvious that it really doesn't need stating. The fact is that very few people do this.

I suspect that this is, partly, out of ignorance - they have no understanding of their own needs or of the benefit of declaring them, - and, partly, out of fear. They do not want to "rock the boat" or they don't want to appear greedy, grasping or demanding!

I do not, however, say "demand your needs". That is where the Trade Unions get it wrong. They talk about "their demands."

I do not think you have to be too deferential either. You simply must recognise that other people have needs, too, and if their needs conflict with yours, then you have something to talk through, and it is very important indeed that you should, even if at the end of the day you agree to differ.

There is no merit at all in burying this conflict under the carpet. It won't go away. All that that will result in is mutual and incomprehensible frustration.

Very often, however, you may find that your needs actually overlap with the other person's, and you have a common interest in meeting them.

So, get your needs out into the open and, equally importantly, encourage other people to do the same. Be explicit. Declaring them doesn't necessarily mean achieving them, but it is at least part of the way there, probably the most important part.

So, here is an exercise for you while I am away.

1. Identify our own three greatest needs and put them in order of importance.
2. Identify your branch's three greatest needs and put them in order of importance.
3. Identify the company's three greatest needs and put them in order of importance.

Decide who best you should communicate these to - and do so! Encourage others to do likewise.

WHAT IS YOUR SERVICE QUALITY

This is an easy letter for me to write! It is a straight copying job! When I was at High Point, North Carolina I came across the following:

WHAT IS YOUR SERVICE QUALITY IQ? A quiz designed by a management consultant to help retailers see the connection between quality and bottom-line profitability.

So here it is.

1. What does poor quality cost a typical home furnishings retailer (as a per cent of total operational costs)?
2. How much more will a typical customer pay to ensure he/she gets higher than average quality in the following products. Automobile Appliance Shoes Suites
3. What is the single biggest turnoff for female shoppers? (Tick one).

   a) Limited selection of merchandise
   b) Unattractive displays
   c) Crowded aisleways ...
   d) Inability to find qualified sales help.

4. What do consumers consider to be the most important component of quality? (Tick one)

   a) Brand name and price ...
   b) Warranty and price
   c) Durability and reliability ...
   d) Multiple options/easy care

5. 'What: are the odds of a customer complaint to your company after purchasing a poor-quality product?

| 1 in 2 | 1 in 3 | 1 in 7 |

6. How many people does a typical customer tell about a bad service experience?
7. How many people does a typical customer tell about a good service experience?
8. Which of the following is not involved in resolving real or perceived mistake? (Tick one)

   -A sincere apology .... showing a sense of urgency .... Offering a special price discount . . . following up to solve

9. Companies that provide "legendary" service do which of the following?

   Concentrate on quality not cost..............Eliminate unnecessary work Do common things uncommonly well ... Communicate excessively

For the answers see over the page. The one justification for making this letter exceed one page in length!

ANSWERS I

1. According to Jerry Epperson, Wheat, First Securities 17%.
2. According to a 1988 Gallup Survey automobiles 21%, appliances 40% shoes 66%, suites 72%.
3. Inability to find qualified sales help.
4. Durability and reliability according to a 1989 survey of 1,000 adult Americans reported in Time Magazine.
5. 1 in 7 according to a 1988 Gallup Survey. (I suspect it is one in three or four with us! It's time we did another check.)
6. About 9-10.
7. About 6.
8. Offering special price discounts
9. All apply.

CURTAINS

Quite a number of our competitors sell curtains - Allied, Maples Storeys and, of course, M&S and departmental stores, and by sell, I mean sell professionally.

We have chosen quite deliberately not to blur our specialist upholstery and bedding niche in the marketplace by including them in our range of merchandise.

I sense, however, that increasingly we have to be prepared to talk about curtains. They are now part of our overall display.

Some upholstery fabrics, especially prints, work very well as curtains or specially co-ordinate with curtains. A professional salesperson asking about a customer's needs will need to be aware of that person's thoughts in relation to curtains. And, if we do sell some fabric there is profit in it.

So, my subject this week is CURTAINS.

It is a world on its own. I know because we used to sell them before we opened the Sunderland Suite Centre. We are into a world of "pencil pleats" "pinch pleats", of "valances" of "pattern match", Of "drop", and how much you allow for fullness and hems, and whether fixed or loose linings are required.

The all-important question, apart from choice of fabric, is how much you need. This needs a professional calculation. The width of the curtain, and therefore the number of widths of fabric overall, depend on the type of heading - it may be anything from half as much again to two and a half times the width of the actual window! The drop must take account of headings, hems, and pattern match.

We prefer the person making up the curtains to make that calculation, but it can be made only if that person knows the width of the material and the pattern match.

What I believe that we must be able to talk about is the effect of the curtains, using the same pattern in the curtains as on the suite, or coordinating plain with pattern, or curtaining an entire wall not just a small window in it, the heading best suited to the material, the valance best suited to the mood of the suite, and maybe even the lighting by fluorescent tube downlighting from behind the pelmet.

I am not suggesting that our sales-staff get deeply involved in all this, but they must have the basic feel of the subject to be confident to comment sensibly about it.

I suggest a training session with John Branskey. He may be able to produce some illustrations to show you the range of possibilities.

THE FOLLOW UP

I hope that you felt that the All-Staff Meeting was a success.

There is no doubt that there was a great atmosphere. How do we make it last? The theme of this letter is THE FOLLOW-UP.

You may have your own ideas about that. I hope you have. Here are my thoughts and suggestions.

Quite apart, from anything that was said, there was a great feeling of fellowship. Don't forget this or underestimate it when you think about the evening.

I first came across the importance of fellowship when I was qualifying as a Barrister. It seemed to be almost as important to wine and dine in an Inn of Court - 36 times in all - than to pass an examination. Then, when I had qualified, there was still more wining and dining in what were called Circuit Dinners. Even though Barristers fight each other in Court, the solidarity of the profession and its standards are established round the dinner-table! And just a little bit of fun at the expense at those who let the side down!

I belong to Rotary, a Club which enable members to contribute service to their communities. The same principle is preached there.

If there is good fellowship in a Club, everything else will follow and individually and collectively good work will be done.

One of the great strengths of SCS lies in the fellowship we generate in the course of a year - Xmas parties and events like our All-Staff Meeting. Don't just take it for granted. Look for opportunities to add to it.

The great theme on the evening was, of course, the contribution that everyone in the company can make to the challenge of the second half of this trading year. How do we make sure we don't lose track of this?

I suggest that you get everyone to write into their diaries on the first day of every month "My contribution to ScS is a real one. It is so important not to underestimate that.

Write into your diary on the last day of every month "Has my team achieved that extra 1%?" If they have, congratulate them. If you don't think they have, do something positive about it.

When everyone is pulling together (hence the fellowship) the sum total of the result is greater than the total of the individual contributions!

That is what we are going to need if we are to reach and pass our company profit target - 5% of turnover!

ENJOYMENT

This week, I would like to pick up one of the themes I talked about at our All-Staff Meeting. I said that I hoped that everyone enjoyed their job, whatever that job was in the company. If we enjoyed selling to our customers, our customers would then enjoy buying from us.

So, the theme of this letter is ENJOYMENT!

I suspect that this isn't something you think much about at all. We take it for granted if it's there. We ignore it - or try to ignore it - if it isn't. That is a pity either way.

So, let's see just how much enjoyment there is in any one week or, better still, one fortnight. I suggest we play a game, and we call the game "Pursuit of Excellence".

It is a game where you can each write the rules and do the scoring. Essentially, the game is to determine just how much enjoyment there is around. All achievements should be enjoyable. Some are greater than others and need to be recognised as such, say from 1 point to 3 points depending on the actual achievement.

To be fair to the situation, you should also knock off the odd point where things go wrong unless you can turn it around to make it work for you. Quite often in life you can turn something bad into something good and, therefore, doubly enjoyable!

I think that everyone must measure their own enjoyment in each case, but you should validate it.

Let's take the salesperson. He makes a sale. That should be enjoyable.

There's a spiff. More enjoyment. An add-on sale. More enjoyment still.

A really difficult sale. More enjoyment still. And, what if he loses a sale? No sadness if every possible effort made and umpteen closes tried. But knock off a point if an opportunity has been missed!

I heard Lendl talking about winning and losing at Tennis. He said that winning was great, but he didn't feel defeat if he had played his very best and still lost! He only felt it if he felt he hadn't done justice to himself. The same should apply in life generally. I would like to see which branch generates the most points. It isn't going to make them the best branch. However, it is all in the mind. And I wouldn't blame that branch for thinking that it was the best branch in the company!

This a competition where the joy is in the playing and the winning not in any prize as it would be a bit unfair to award one in a competition with such ill-defined rules and where the results could be so enjoyably rigged!

I am enclosing a self-assessment job enjoyment form for each member of your team. I look forward to hearing the results.

BLINKERS!

No-one likes to criticise, still less to be criticised. Maybe that is one reason why people shy away from being critical, as though that was the first stage in any criticism.

Looking at a situation critically simply means looking at it analytically and with an open mind? So, putting it another way, my subject this week is BLINKERS! How do you get rid of them?

First, you need time. Instant judgments are not only useless. They are positively dangerous. Blinkers! You think you have considered something when you haven't even started to.

Secondly, you need to decide what the question is. If you ask the wrong question, even the right answer won't be much help. Blinkers again!

Thirdly, you need to assemble the facts - as many as possible to begin with, and then the really relevant ones.

Fourthly, you need background information.

Fifthly, you must stand back and make sure you include yourself in the situation you are trying to understand.

Without all this, blinkers again!

Now, you need not just time, but undisturbed time to think. Relax! Let your brain do the work for you. If it is all tensed up, your thoughts will simply go round in tiny circles. Make sure you have a pencil and a pad for those random thoughts which should start flowing. After a while, start to organize them logically and maybe more thoughts will follow.

You finally have to decide what needs doing, how it should be done, and when it should be done. "What", "how" and "when" are different questions. Respect the difference.

I hope I don't have to spend too much time here suggesting topics for critical analysis. Obviously "are we selling enough?" are we selling profitably enough? is our advertising cost effective? are the sort of questions that you should be putting to yourself on a regular basis - not just when someone else asks you to!

I am not inviting you to "chew the cud". When you see a sheep apparently munching the same piece of grass for hours on end, you see what you have to avoid.

The important thing to realise that the scene is constantly changing. Your thinking has to reflect that. If you start with your former conclusion, you really are wasting your time. Blinkers! You may, however, end up confirming it and that's fine.

Axiom for the week: good managers never, never wear blinkers!

ACHIEVERS

I found myself watching a program on the box entitled ACHIEVERS. I commend the series to you and I make this my topic for the week. The hero, or more properly, the heroine of the piece was a lady selling buckets! They were industrial buckets that were part of giant earth moving equipment, not in other words buckets of the domestic kind.

She certainly deserved to be labeled an "achiever". She used language that was clearcut and positive. She didn't talk about thinking. She talked about putting "her intelligent head" on. She certainly didn't wear blinkers! She recognised that she could not live on past successes and that she was only as good as her last job and the next. She talked about the absolute imperative of honouring commitments made to her customers.

She focused on building personal relationships with her customers that would stand the odd thing going wrong, because she was personally committed to putting it right.' As she said, even if she got the price wrong, the personal relationship with her customers would keep the business relationship going. Remember, Richard Denny. People buy people. People certainly buy that lady!

And she sold buckets by knowing what her customers wanted from them and delivering it. It wasn't just a question of - here's a bucket, buy it! She was out in the field, finding out what her customers wanted and relaying it back to the factory so that they could make it.

Above all, she believed in herself, and she was totally dedicated to success. She was a bonny fighter, a very bonny fighter!

So far as I could see, there was no hole in her bucket! I would not like to sell buckets against her!

She's certainly an "achiever". I like the word "achiever" in a business setting. It is open to anyone to be one.

What happens, however, when he is not? I suppose that means that if someone is a non-achiever" or a "not-very-much achiever" then, there is "not—very—much" to be said for it!

Being an "achiever", however, is not an abstract concept. You cannot be an achiever without achievements on an on-going basis! No-one can kid themselves that they are achievers without them.

I hope that this letter may enable you to frame a question relevant to your branch where you can apply the analytical approach I set out in my last letter.

As I said at the outset of that letter, this is not to lead into criticism or self-criticism but into a better understanding of what is going on.

MARGINS

I don't suppose the name Bertie Payne means anything to you. He died a while ago, but in his later years he was a travelling consultant for the National Association of Retail Furnishers. When I was very raw at the game, I remember him for two pieces of advice. The first was to sign my letters "Managing Director" and the other was not to give discounts!

Steve has asked me to write about gross and net margins and Bertie Payne's advice to me over 20 years ago is as good a starting point as any in this week's topic MARGINS.

At the time of his visit, "discounting" was becoming more and more fashionable, and it did look as though he was playing the role of King Canute trying to turn back the tide. However, the essential point that he made was a valid one and does bear thinking about. What he said was this: if you are targeting a net profit of 10%, on a £1,000 order that is £100. If you give that away in discount to make the sale, you are effectively sacrificing the net profit on that sale, and you will have to generate it from some other sale.

Obviously, every sale we make with some gross profit margin helps to pay our expenses, but if our objective is to generate 5% or more net profit then we should understand just what is happening when we "buy business" and the price we are paying for it.

The same logic also applies when it comes to the cost of after- sales service and its effect on profit. There will always be a need for service, but if there is a weakness in a suite or a weakness in our handling it which requires after-sales service we are losing the net profit on the sale of that suite. The average cost of servicing, conservatively, is about 5% of our average suite price! Ironically, it costs about the same amount of money in our advertising to secure each sale in the first place.

So, if we are talking about bottom line profit and not turnover, the real opportunity to generate it comes in three distinct ways:

1. Generating sales without any advertising costs immediately generates more bottom-line profit. Using business cards, securing recommendations, building on satisfied customers must be a high priority and acknowledging those who get sales that way.
2. No-one wants to turn business away but do know what you are doing when you offer a discount. Remember Bertie Payne! The professional salesperson gets the sale on his terms not his customers!
3. If you can do anything to head off a service problem before it happens - remember the costs of the horror saga Mike brought to our all staff meeting and, again more bottom-line profit.

So, if you go back to letter no. 28, you may feel that here are three more questions for your critical attention.

FIRST IMPRESSIONS

FIRST IMPRESSIONS

We often talk about first impressions, but do we really consider all that the eye takes in during the first 10 or 20 seconds.

I am not talking about just the first impressions people form when they walk into an SCS branch. I am talking about the first impressions people form in relation to any experience of SCS noticing an SCS advert can be a first impression of the company-meeting someone who works for SCS in a pub, likewise. When the van drives up delivering a new suite, there will be a first impression of that aspect of the company's activity, or when you see the van in the Street.

There is no doubt in my mind that the thing that people notice the most is not the thing that is right, but the thing that is wrong. The "sore thumb" It is unfair to all the good things around, but that is the way the world works.

The badly scratched coffee table cheapens the suite it stands besides no matter how beautiful the suite. The dirty van condemns the company, likewise the driver not smartly dressed. (This is not a backdoor route to criticising anyone!) The first words spoken on a telephone, the appearance of sales staff and what they are doing when you walk into a branch, the pricing of the suites and their relationship to the current offer, the way in which point of sale display is presented, the condition of the paintwork, the carpet, the windows, the bits of litter.

It is always the little things!

It is crazy, but the badly knotted tie, the shoes that don't match the socks, the coffee stain, the "it's been a long hard day" look, the "I'm just about to close" look. All these things construct obstacles between you and your customer. So, first you construct them and then you have to climb over them before you can start really relating to your customer.

It must be better to avoid them in the first place.

How do you do that? Very simple. Instinctively, look for the things that are wrong, however small. In fact, especially when they are small! This isn't something you do once a quarter or once a month. There is no escape from it. You have to do it all the time. You must set a standard and then maintain it. No one else is going to do it for you!

When you know someone well, you don't see the warts. So, you must look at everything as though you are seeing it for the first time.

Make a start. Make yourself a check list of the things that could be wrong. Write it permanently into your diary.

Then, just close your eyes, open them, and look around.

TEAMWORK

Once again, this week's theme has been provided by a management programme on the box. It does pay to look out for them and watch them. The theme, this week, is TEAMWORK.

Like so many other things, you take it for granted when it is there, and you don't quite notice its absence when it is not. And yet it is of the absolute essence to success.

Today, you can do nothing on your own. I repeat that, and I am tempted to go on repeating it to the bottom of the page because it is so important. You can do nothing on your own. You need other people's knowledge and expertise. You need other people's efforts and energies. You need other people's eyes and ears. You need other people's commitment. It is not a sign of weakness to ask for it!

It is an arrogance to believe or act as though it were not the case!

Look at a racing eight on a river. The oarsmen not looking where they are going and a diminutive cox, who can't see where they are going, driving them on. It looks like a formula for disaster. And it is if one of the oarsmen "catches a crab". However, by training and dedication and teamwork, it works.

Any group of 'people' can constitute a team provided they have a singleness of purpose and a will to succeed. They also need a team leader - not a dictator, not an Emperor or a King, but a first among equals. This is a very old concept going back to Roman times! They called it "primus inter pares". There must be some use for my old Latin!

When you have got a team working with you, the members of the team don't just think of themselves and their own needs, they think of the needs of their colleagues and of the team itself and they help each other. You can see and feel when this is happening, and you can usually see and feel when it is not! "Quality circles" have been introduced into industry to harness this to secure consistently high quality.

This, of course, is one of the great strengths of Japanese approach. Their commitment to the group, and beyond it to the organisation and beyond that to Japan Inc. is extraordinarily successful. People do increasingly recognise, however, from Japanese experience, that you do have to be careful to ensure that the group is not so disciplined that it stifles individual initiative and so hierarchical that it stands in the way of youthful enthusiasm.

You may recall that I suggested that you might think about these letters in the bath or driving to work or during a walk.

This is one of those subjects worth mulling over in this way. If you are leading, be sure that if you look over your shoulder, someone is there!

WORRY

I have been asked to devote one of these letters to WORRY! I hope that that is not a worrying matter so far as the person suggesting it is concerned. I don't think that it is. It is clearly worth writing about. Worry can create stress and whilst stress can in short bursts get the adrenalin going, when it is unmanaged and uncontrolled and on-going, it can sap energy and reduce effectiveness.

A wise man said - I don't know his name - "Some of the griefs you have cured and the sharpest you have survived, but what torments of pain you endured ... from evils that never arrived." In short, much worry is unfounded! The problem is to identify it. Of course, some people are born worriers. "Should I, or shouldn't I?" "Will he, or won't he?" "Is he annoyed, or isn't he?" "How annoyed?" "Should I apologise?" "Or shouldn't I?" Their fingernails are down to the quick.

You can't say to these people "Stop worrying." They wouldn't know what to do with themselves. You could give them some worry beads, but that will only encourage them to worry some more.

So, what do you say to them?

Simply say "What are you worried about?", not "What are you worried about?" You may think that the worry is more imaginary than real, but the person concerned won't think so. Then, encourage the person to talk it through to a conclusion..., his conclusion or yours, but don't leave it up in the air. The worrying will go on unabated.

There are, of course, some very real worries. Health must rank as the most important. Fear of the unknown is much worse than knowledge of the known. Bereavement in a family can leave those most closely affected with trauma. In these situations, professional advice and counselling is the right thing to suggest but showing real sympathy and understanding will help.

Worry at work is obviously another possible area of anxiety. This may be associated with worry about money. This sort of worry feeds upon itself. A sportsman loses form. A gambler loses his luck. It doesn't help simply to say, "Try a little harder". Trying can be counterproductive. I know this with my approach shots at golf! The harder I try, the more I tense up and the worse the shot!

Somehow or other you must relax with the problem. Be a bit philosophical about it. Get it into perspective. See that as worries go, it's far from the worst - yours or other people's for that matter. The story is told of a group of people, all with problems, worries and sadnesses who came together and were invited to put their problem or worry into the middle and exchange it for one of the others. Everyone preferred to take back their own!

Essentially, I believe that a worry shared is a worry halved.

THE LAW

As you probably know, many years ago I qualified as a lawyer. Today, my knowledge is not just rusty. It is corroded. I have, however, been left with a few conditioned "legal" reflexes and I want to put some of them down here this week. So, my subject is THE LAW!

The first reflex is to keep away from it - it is very time-consuming and money consuming as well. The main beneficiaries are the lawyers!

If you want to keep away from it, you must understand what it is and, more importantly, what it isn't.

It is a set of rules. Those rules govern relationships trying to strike a balance between the strong and the weak, the buyer and the seller, the landlord and the tenant, the employer, and the employee (civil law) - and people generally the State, and the individual (criminal law).

Although you might like to think that the Law is just, it is never quite going to be that because different people have a different idea of what is and what is not just. So, it is not a matter of what ought or ought not to happen. It is a matter of what the rules say should or should not happen.

Ignorance of the rules is no defense in a Court of Law ... or in SCS! It is not very clever starting a game of cricket if you don't know the precise way the lbw rule operates!

It is your professional business to know what the rules are. If you don't know, then you must ask! Sales of Goods, Health & Safety, Bargain Offer legislation, Employment protection, Flammability &c.

The second reflex is to put important matters in relation to all contracts into writing as soon as they happen. If you want to reserve your position, then mark the paper "without prejudice". If you want to be in a position to confirm the dispatch of a document, send it "by recorded delivery". The third reflex is don't jump to a conclusion. Find out all the facts first and, if necessary, take advice. It is cheaper to take advice early on than later!

If we decide to go to court, we do have a policy of insurance covering our legal costs, but the insurance company must be alerted to the possibility of legal proceedings taken either by us or against us just as soon as we sense that this might happen.

It takes two to Tango. It takes two to go to Court! Quite often both sides contribute one way or another to it happening. A short cut, an ambiguity in an arrangement, an oversight, taking a chance, stubbornness, or just plain ignorance can all contribute.

So, only one exercise this week. Do you know the rules?

SPEED

I have written about "Tempo", and I have written about "Pace", letters No.1 and 6. 1 made the point that neither of these words meant speed. I suggest you refresh your memory about their meanings before you proceed further, because this week my theme is SPEED.

Three things have provoked me to write about this. First, I heard an architect responsible for the new swimming baths in Sheffield prepared for the World Student Games talking in terms of a "fast pool". Now, in my simple ignorance, I could not credit that there was such a thing. Water is the water wherever it is. Then, I am a slow swimmer! I did not recognise the "drag" effect of the ripples going out to the side of the baths and then coming back again and going to the bottom and coining up again. Make the pool longer, wider and deeper with the regulation distances within that and, hey presto, more British records have been broken in that pool in the last two months than in the rest of the century! (Note: improved working environment leads to improved performance.)

A bit of professional design work – North-East based, I am pleased to say - and, swimmers will flock to Sheffield, because that's where they can swim fastest and that is what the real swimmers always aspire to do. The professional is never satisfied in any activity.

Secondly, I have just heard that a few more precious minutes have been lopped off Intercity journeys between Durham and King's Cross and with electrification this autumn the journey will get even quicker. A 7.13 a.m. start instead of 7a.m. is certainly good news for me.

Lastly, Karen asked how we managed in the days before Fax.

Instinctively, man does want constantly to move faster and, in consequence, achieve more. With forward planning, budgets, timetables, deadlines we "ski", maybe "slalom" is a better word, through life at ever increasing speeds and in business there really is no alternative. You can't fight it, and you shouldn't fight it.

You do have to recognise this, accept it, and understand that unless you also "pace" your life with pauses for breath and refreshment there is a "wear and tear" factor, "a stress and strain" factor that can be quite destructive of the quality of work and the quality of life as well!

Fresh air, assuming you can find it, and exercise, assuming you are up to it and relaxation, assuming you know how to, should be quite deliberately built into the pattern of each week's activities.

Then, when you want to accelerate you will have the reserve of will and energy to do so and will enjoy it!

Exercise for this week; stop and think or, at least for a brief moment, sit down, relax and put your feet up!

INITIATIVE & RESOURCEFULLNESS

I sometimes discuss the themes of these letters with people I meet. I was in London recently and was sitting outside a pub one lunchtime. I was just saying how some people didn't ever seem to expect "Murphy" and were totally surprised when he appeared, when my attention was drawn to a van rolling by with "Murphy & Sons" emblazoned on its side! What a brazen chap he is! So, you don't just have to look out for Murphy these days. You must watch out for his sons as well!

I was talking to an old school friend, currently an anaesthetist in Haifa and, in the course of that conversation, I said how important I felt "winning the tempo" was in life, Letter No.1. He said he understood what I was getting at because the Israeli army, which has quite a reputation as a citizen army, preaches to all its conscripts the crucial importance of INITIATIVE AND RESOURCEFULNESS and that is my theme for this week.

It is unusual for any army to urge this. Usually, armies are trained in obedience to orders and discipline. That's one way of heading off retreat and surrender - one option the Israelis don't really have.

What about, however, initiative and resourcefulness in a business setting? There is no doubt that these ought to be buzz words especially when you come to generating sales and dealing with consumer situations.

It is all very well looking at the rule book, but that is based on yesterdays' situations not on today's.

So, what are the key factors in taking initiatives and being resourceful? First, courage! One part of being an entrepreneur - Letter No.22 Secondly, imagination - Letter No. 28 Blinkers. Thirdly, persuasiveness. It's no good having good ideas if you can't carry people with them. Lastly, persistence. It is very important not to give up on a good idea. Try presenting it better, implementing it better, or just getting the timing right.

All of this is not just a management skill, it is a life skill. Absolutely anyone can show initiative and resourcefulness and should be positively encouraged to do so.

Entebbe here we come!

A recession is a challenging time. In a strange way, it is an opportunistic time as weaker companies fall by the wayside or "retrench" awaiting better times. We can turn this to our advantage.

Exercise: how far do you and your staff recognise all this?

WINNING FORMULA

As you may know, I chair the Furniture and Carpet Industry Action Group responding to the Office of Fair Trading's criticisms of the Industry. We have just about finished our development work. I hope that in the coming months you are going to hear a lot about "Qualitas" and what it stands for - essentially, an assurance of quality service in our industry - "Qualitas" being to us what "St. Michael" is to M&S, a brand to take a pride in and to promote.

I was asked to provide a quote summing it all up.

Here it is "Old fashioned values, professionalism, and teamwork - a great mix". I suddenly realised that this was our WINNING FORMULA, too!

Businesses today are encouraged to write a mission statement for themselves, so that everyone knows where they are going. I am sure that this would be a very important part of ours. "Old fashioned values" - gardeners might prefer to call them perennial values - is not just about quality and service. It is about personal integrity, making promises and keeping your word.

Professionalism is about fine detail. It involves being prepared to pay for it.' It is rarely cheap on money or time! It involves accepting that yesterday's ways may no longer be either good enough or appropriate either.

Teamwork. Well, I have dealt with that in Letter 32. It is so important to draw on the know-how of lots of people and make it all work together, the sum total being greater than the individual parts taken separately.

Overall, there must be a recognition of interdependence. We have to recognise that we depend on our suppliers and they have to recognise that they depend on us. Both we and our suppliers must recognise that we depend on our customers, but they for their part depend on us!

This is not a very original idea. M&S have been operating on this basis very successfully for years.

Essentially, it means getting away from the "us" and "them" approach to life with all its conflicts and confrontations. It is very time-wasting and energy draining. If you think about it, people have more things in life that unite them and divide them.

Exercise: read the final report of the Furniture & Carpet Industry Action Group and tell me what you think. It is, after all, a "Consultative" document. I very much want your considered thoughts.

CRITICISM

"Would that God, the gift would give us, to see ourselves as others see us." My apologies to the Scots for not putting this into the authentic original.

My topic, this week, is CRITICISM. I am provoked to write about it because of a number of meetings with people involved in education. The point was made to me that the public service sector really does run a mile from provoking criticism, whilst private enterprise actively encourages it, seeing in criticism the way to improve.

Is this comparison legitimate?

Some might say that no one likes to be criticised, but is it as simple as that?

Certainly, no-one likes to be criticised publicly, no-one likes to be criticised unfairly, no-one likes to be criticised if it in any way implies lack of integrity, and no-one likes to be criticised without being given an opportunity to reply and maybe explain.

No-one likes it if there is only criticism and never praise!

The words used are relevant, "Stupid", "Cretin", "Idiot" may be what you feel provoked to say, and indeed should say to get the criticism home, but these words should be used with proper thought beforehand not off the top of your head, without thinking about the effect. You may be able to get away with them if there is no-one about, and you have a sad smile on your face!

The tone of voice is relevant. Cold anger is more powerful than hot temper. Usually, you should show feelings not hide them, but if you show them, you should also control them! And, you have got to be prepared for other people to show theirs to you.

What I am saying here is relevant whether you are on the giving end or on the receiving end of criticism.

Two things are most important. Criticism for criticisms sake is not very helpful to anyone. It must be with a view to improving matters. Secondly, criticism that rumbles on is not very helpful either.

Lastly, as I say quite often, if the matter is important and you don't want to forget about it altogether, confirm the criticism in writing and it is then on the record. If the situation should recur, you are not back at square one again. However, by putting it into writing, tactfully, (amid who types the letter is relevant), you may help to prevent it recurring.

There are no specific exercises this week. I don't want you to go out and practice unless you absolutely must!

RESPONDING TO CRITICISM

Having written last week about criticism, it is only right that I should write this week about how to deal with it! So, my subject this week is RESPONDING TO CRITICISM.

The first thing you must do is to listen to it. The second, to take a deep breath!

In order to deal with criticism, you have to understand fully what has provoked it. It may be nothing to do with you at all. It may be because the person criticising is having a bad day, or had a bad night, or was himself the subject of someone else's criticism and is looking for a scapegoat.

On the other hand, you may just have provoked it yourself!

The first thing you must decide is how and, importantly, when to respond. You may want to find out some facts first. You may want to choose a quiet moment at the beginning or preferably at the end of a day. It may be better over a glass of beer.

If there is any heat in the situation, it may be all the more important to let matters cool down. Playing for time may be a good defensive technique, as long as you don't try to play for too much time.

The word people tend to use in relation to criticism is "parry" it.

That is very different from running for cover. It involves the giving of an answer. On TV, politicians are adept at parrying criticism by answering one question with an answer to some quite different question that has never been asked in the first place, but which the politician would have much preferred. I do not recommend this in a business setting.

However, if you have really listened to the criticism, fully understand what lies beneath it, then you will be best able to deal with it constructively. Any other way simply postpones the day of reckoning.

What about replying to a criticism with a criticism? That may be the right thing to do. You may be criticised for not doing a job. You may not have been given the tools! or the time!

If it is that kind of situation, it is by far the best thing to get the whole argument out into the open. Don't just seethe!

And, if you can't agree - everyone doesn't have to agree with everyone else all the time - call in an arbitrator to get it decided one way or another. Who is the arbitrator? Someone both respect for his judgment.

Of course, if the worst comes to the worst you can apologise! It is not a sign of weakness. It is simply an acceptance of human fallibility! Yours! Again, I hope there is no exercise this week.

POOR QUALITY

Who is John David Stanhope? Why do I ask? I was looking at an advertisement for Rover Cars, and at the top of it came the following "Confused about price cuts? 'The bitter taste of poor quality remains long after the sweet taste of low price is forgotten.' John David Stanhope."

Whoever he is, and if anyone can tell me I would be grateful, he deserves a medal. In one short sentence, he has summed up the choice that people have to make in the marketplace.

We talk about quality and how important it is. We don't sufficiently talk about POOR QUALITY and how disastrous it is. It is worth looking at quality that way round for a change, and that is my topic for this week.

It is not surprising, of course, that this quote comes from a British carmaker. Many years ago, British-made was synonymous with quality. Then, the carmaker took the view that it was cheaper to build a car without quality control and put right any faults during the warranty period. So, little things went wrong. We all know what they were and how irritating to have to deal with them in a prized new possession. It spoiled the pleasure and ruined a journey.

The Japanese then came on the scene, and I believe that Mazda boasted warranty claims of less than £1 a car. Not surprisingly they made inroads into the market.

Furniture has not been so very different. Fortunately - at least for our manufacturers - Japanese don't sit on suites, and haven't got round to making them.

If, however, quite a number of furniture buyers don't get the pleasure they expect from a major new purchase and only share their woes with their friends, it should not be too surprising if their friends choose to spend their money on something more reliable.

So often it is the little irritant, and remember an irritant is something that annoys over a period of time.' The stone in a shoe may be tiny, but it pains whilst it is there. The grit in the eye pains even after you have removed it! It isn't just the big defect.

The law will soon echo this, because changes to the Sale of Goods Act are under way that will make it a term of every contract of sale that goods are "free from minor defects."

Poor quality in essence comes from people failing to set proper standards, failing to reject second best and start again, failing to have the patience, or even the arrogance to ask for the best. Poor quality happens because it is allowed to happen. It is tolerated, excused or, worse, not even noticed.

Exercise: do we plead "guilty or not guilty"? or do you rely on the Scottish verdict "not proven"?

ADVERSITY

I have a thing about hotel bedrooms. It's not that it's usually more comfortable to be at home. It's just that it doesn't take much to stop me sleeping - the snoring of a travelling companion being the worst offender, but the noise and vibration of passing traffic, the band downstairs, and thin plaster walls that talk incomprehensibly being others.

What provokes me to write about this now? I was staying at the Holiday Inn in Manchester for this year's G.Mex when, just as I was about to switch off the light, I heard a drip, quickly followed by another and another. I was not on the top floor, and, in any event, it wasn't raining! My first thought was that someone was having a very full bath.

My subject this week is how management should tackle ADVERSITY.

I am not here talking about my adversity - I suppose earplugs might have been the answer - but that of the management of the Holiday Inn.

After I called Reception, a porter emerged and said that it was the air conditioning, that it was not the first time - not much comfort to me - and offered a bucket and a towel under the leak. Also, not much comfort to me!

Then, the Manager came on the 'phone making the same offer, which I gently declined. I was surprised by my own gentleness. I asked for a change of room. He indicated that the hotel was full, but he could move me to a hotel in North Manchester. Again, I gently declined. He also offered me a rebate, which was not what I was after at all. What I wanted was a night's rest. Without all that much hope I then firmly demanded a plumber. I do know that plumbers are not all that easy to get hold of during the day. let alone at one o'clock in the morning.

It was then that the situation took a major turn for the better. The night manager arrived on the scene with the porter, a screwdriver, and a wastepaper basket! I must hand it to the manager. He did not delegate the job to the porter! I think he knew what was coming, as he removed his jacket before climbing on to a chair, removing the tile and exposing the air conditioning plant.

He released a screw, and a sudden downpour drenched him thoroughly with a small amount of water going into the wastepaper basket. The leaking stopped, and I suddenly felt a warm glow of appreciation coupled with some sympathy for his wet predicament.

I am sure that you have got the message. First, in the face of adversity, there is often no substitute for prompt and effective action by you without leaving it to anyone else. Also, you cannot buy yourself out of every untoward situation and you shouldn't even try. A waste of time and money!

I hope this doesn't cause you too many sleepless nights!

ZERO DEFECTS
– NO SUCH THING

I have been talking about poor quality, then adversity and what you should do about them. I propose to continue in the same vein. My subject this week is disaster - or, better expressed as ZERO DEFECTS - NO SUCH THING.

I recently read an interesting tale about Club Medcancum, part of Paris based Club Mediterranee. A party of holiday makers had nothing but trouble getting from New York to their Mexican destination.

Their flight took off 6 hours late, made 2 unexpected stops, and circled for 30 minutes before it could land. The plane was en route for 10 hours longer than planned and ran out of food and drinks. It finally landed at 2 o'clock in the morning, with a landing so rough that oxygen masks had to be used and luggage dropped from overhead. By the time the plane landed, the soured passengers were faint with hunger and convinced that their holiday was ruined before it had even started. One lawyer on board was already collecting names and addresses for a lawsuit.

The general manager of the resort got word of the horrendous flight. He had a name throughout the organisation for his ability to satisfy customers. He immediately took half of his staff to the airport where they laid out a table of snacks and drinks and set up a stereo system to play lively music.

As the guests filed through the gate they received personal greetings, help with their bags, a sympathetic ear and a chauffeured ride to the resort. Waiting for them at the Club Med was a lavish banquet, complete with mariachi band and champagne. The staff had rallied other guests to wait up and greet the newcomers, and the partying continued until sunrise. Many guests said that it was the most fun they'd had since college.

I'm sure you have got the message. Don't run away from disaster. Don't pretend it didn't happen. Don't try and forget that it did.

Of course, it's not too difficult to forget it as long as you are not one of the casualties. You should resist the temptation.

The truth is that you should be ready for things going wrong, because there's no such thing as "zero defects" and "idiot proof" even in SCS.

Make sure that you personally have a good early warning system. Use it to plan your "recovery situation." Remember the casualty will talk about the things that have gone wrong unless you give them something very much better.

You have no idea how much satisfaction comes from turning a situation that has gone badly wrong into another situation where it is actually better than if it had gone smoothly in the first place. You should also help to solve problems that are not of our making.

So, don't look the other way, pretend it hasn't happened, pray for forgiveness but do nothing, or just "duck"!

Exercise this week: make sure everyone understands the choice!

DURABILITY

I recently came across this description of Wartime and immediately post-War Utility Furniture: "This stuff is here for your correction, although it fails to stir affection." This provoked me to compose the following in relation to the furniture we buy and sell today:

"This gear is here for your delight, and as for lasting, well, it might. My subject this week is DURABILITY!

In letter no.40 I said that changes were under way to make it a term of contract that goods should be "free from minor defects." Another change will be a requirement that goods should be "durable".

What is "durable"? Or more precisely, how long is "durable"? We increasingly live in a "throw-away" society. More and more things are "disposable" because it is easier and cheaper to replace than repair. Also, fashion beckons and, it buries.

On the other hand, there are occasions when people still want things to last, and it should be their choice when they are fed up with them rather than the manufacturer's by building in weaknesses that will render them obsolescent.

So, how do we give people what they want?

The answer is that we must match the manufacturer's suggested use with the consumer's expected use. The professional salesperson will have been doing this for years quite naturally, finding out what the customer really needs and then trying to meet that need, and if there is any special need, making sure that it is accurately recorded both for the customer and for the manufacturer.

Many sales, however, as I'm sure you agree, are not made that way!

It is for that reason that part of the Qualitas package deals with product information...The object is to get the manufacturer, preferably on the basis of British Standard tests, to say what use he recommends for his furniture - Occasional, Light, General or Heavy. Some carpet manufacturers already do this relating the carpet to the room in the house and defining it as to Light, Medium, Heavy and Extra heavy.

This helps the customer make a sensible choice. It also helps the retailer and supplier by providing a yardstick for "durability" in relation to use. That has to be the principal factor in determining whether or not a product has performed properly.

All being well, next Spring our suites will all carry this information. In the meantime, when you are selling a print suite or a sofa bed or any suite for that matter, just remember that what Qualitas is setting out is what the good and responsible salespeople have been doing for years without it!

LADY LUCK

Last night I heard some very sad news, that Barry Myers had taken his own life.

I have been thinking about writing a letter about luck, and this is probably as right a time as any to do so.

So here it is - LADY LUCK. Why "lady"? Because it is just so unpredictable, and it can be good, and it can be bad. I hope that this is not too "male chauvinist" a remark.

I occasionally play a game of poker - very high stakes, all of 5p - and one particular person always seems to have two aces above my two kings, Threes over my two pairs, and fours over my full house! In life, sometimes you can feel that the cards are stacked against you.

This is how it seemed to be with Barry. Business, marriage, business again and health kept striking him down. Each time, he came back fighting, and that's really all that you can do when things go badly wrong. And, I guess to take your own life takes a kind of courage, too!

He was a kind, considerate and gentle man. He knew a lot about upholstered furniture, too. In today's tough competitive world that was just not enough.

That was his luck.

Ironically, there would be no SCS and Mike and I would never have teamed up without Barry, and that was ours!

Way back in the early 1970's, it was Barry and his brother-in-law Philip who urged me to start selling suites - as distinct from playing around with furniture - and to get a manager to help me to do so. It was Barry who helped to draw up a list of retailers around the country for me to visit - an early Queensway, Kingsway, Oakhives in Kent, Haskins in the West Country - all of whom were "motoring" their sales. It was Barry and Philip who introduced me to Mike and Mike to me.

The moral of the story - when you are fortunate enough to get some good luck, grab it with both hands. It doesn't come every day and it doesn't come to everyone.

People say you make your own luck. I don't entirely agree. You need a bit to make a bit. Barry's ran out quite a long time ago.

I know that he had many friends in this company, and I shall be passing on their sympathy as well as my own to his family.

ONE WRONG WORD

ONE WRONG WORD! It is always dangerous apologising for something. The recipient of the apology may not realise the error until the apology arrives! That happened to me once with quite serious consequences at the time.

However, the danger must be faced, because so many lessons can be learnt from that one wrong word".

So, what I am talking about? Well, I showed Ros my letter in relation to Barry Myers' death. She took great exception to my reference to "Lady" luck! "Men", she said "can exhibit exactly the same trait of unpredictability as women, and they can be equally good and bad too. Whether I liked it or not, it was a sexist remark, and the fact that other people used the words "Lady luck" was not sufficient reason for my doing so as well.

I have got my letters a bit out of synch at the moment, letters no.38 to 43 written, but not yet circulated. Ironically, the next two are entitled "Criticism" and "Responding to Criticism"!

So, I here give you the illustration before the narrative.

I conclude the second with the following "Of course, if the worst comes to the worst you can apologise! It is not a sign of weakness. It is simply an acceptance of human fallibility." So, I do apologise.

And letter no 42 is relevant as well. "You have no idea how much satisfaction comes from turning a situation that has gone badly wrong into another situation where it is actually better than if it had gone smoothly in the first place."

That is what I would now like to attempt!

There are at least three important lessons to be learnt here.

1. Male chauvinism or male arrogance can be very upsetting to the female. We may think of it as being somewhat humorous, but if you are on the receiving end, you don't like it. Am I the only culprit here?
2. I have urged you to put things into writing. That's fine as long as you get the wording right. Even if one word is wrong the purpose of the letter can be ruined. A good adage is "if in doubt, leave it out." Sometimes you have to tear up a letter and start again. When did you last do that?
3. Lesley read my letter before it went out. Did she spot the error, but was too polite, deferential to point it out to me? She should, in the nicest possible way, have tried to do so. She should feel that she can criticise. Do your office staff feel that it is safe to suggest alterations to your letters?

"There but for the grace of God go I." As you read this, do you agree?

LUCK CONTD

- Well, Lesley didn't think that there was anything wrong with "Lady" luck. She just doesn't believe in luck in that sense at all. Mind you she didn't express this contrary view to mine until I asked for it. Maybe she will next tame.

This week, the theme is LUCK CONTD.

Lesley believes that you make your own. I should have anticipated that that would have been her very positive view. She quite rightly feels that she is not where she is today because of luck but hard work and commitment, and SCS, too, for that matter would not be where it is but for the commitment of all those involved in it.

I might still say that she has simply done what I said and that is grabbed the opportunity when it was presented, call that luck if you like. Some people don't recognise an opportunity when they see one, whatever you want to call it.

Of course, the problem with relying on the word luck to explain things is that it can very easily be nothing more nor less than an alibi for failure.

Bad luck to miss a sale when it was bad salesman ship. Bad luck that the suite failed to meet a promised date when no-one checked that it did. Bad luck that a suite had just a tiny fault which that very "fussy" customer spotted, even though similar faults had already shown themselves. Bad luck that the second suite was also faulty and the sale lost, when it could have been checked. Bad luck that the customer was out when no-one made sure that the customer was in. Just very bad luck-we didn't hit our targets.

And, likewise, good fortune is attributed to someone's good luck rather than to that person's hard work, expertise, commitment, and personal ambition. There is something just a little un-British in having too much of any of these things. Better, therefore, say that the rewards are a bit like a win on the Pools! Wait long enough and it might happen to you.

Statistically, it is a very long time!

People in other countries, and especially Japan, Germany, the US, and Hong Kong, just don't appear to leave things to luck at all!

So, maybe Lesley is right about "luck" and Ros was right about "lady" and the sooner that I change the subject the better.

Maybe, letters nos. 44, 45, 46 should all go under the single heading of "wastepaper basket". On second thoughts, file them with the rest as a gentle reminder of two very important truths, first that you should not assume you are always right and secondly you should check out what other people think - especially wives and secretaries!

ASSERTIVENESS

In letter No. 46 I said that it was very important to check out what other people think. There are all sorts of reasons for doing this. First, you yourself may just be wrong, secondly, you may not be wrong, but you could be better, thirdly to ask someone else's opinion may help your relationship with that other person and have real merit on that account, provided of course you genuinely want to hear it.

I want to write this letter about ASSERTIVENESS, but to look at it the opposite way round from the way I and many others, I suspect, usually look at it.

There is a widespread view that many people, and especially women, don't know how to stand up for themselves, how to say what they really feel and think, and, putting it bluntly, how on occasion to say "NO".

Yet whose problem is this? Certainly, they will feel it is their problem, but the real problem lies with the person denying them their freedom of expression. In a way, he is in greater need of "training" than anyone on the receiving end of "assertiveness training", because he doesn't even see and recognise that there is a problem in the first place!

It is a cliche to say that in any society or organisation there is a "pecking order". Most people spend part of their time "being pecked" and another part of their time "pecking"!

So, it's not a bad idea trying to understand what "pecking" is all about.

The great "Pecker" of our generation was undoubtedly Margaret Thatcher. No-one needed to teach her assertiveness! Or did they?

She did her best to surround herself with people who were eminently "peckable"! It worked, in a manner of speaking, for 11 years! And, then Michael Heseltine, Geoffrey Howe and Nigel Lawson "pecked" the hen.

The truth is that "peckers" can be too assertive or not assertive enough, too assertive if they drown all comment and criticism, not assertiveness enough if they don't declare their own needs clearly and unambiguously.

This is where the problem really starts. It is compounded if the "pecked" do any one of a number of things - suffer in silence, secretly retaliate (a long time ago I once witnessed a sorry sight of a chief executive being "filleted by Phyllis" simply excluding him from her territory) or conspire with others in passive resistance!

Of course, in today's complicated business world, you just never know where the next "peck" is coming from! No wonder birds have eyes in the sides of their heads and keep moving!

My advice to the "pecker" is very simple: Do as you would be done by! And, to the "pecked", find a sympathetic and helpful management ear.

STREET-WISE

A few months ago, John Major ruffled a few feathers in the world of education by saying that he felt that the lessons that life can provide can be better than book learning.

Looking at this in a purely business setting I don't disagree even though this is something of an indictment of would-be whizz kids currently involved with courses in business management and administration.

Most importantly, education doesn't make people STREET WISE, only experience and "learnt from" experience can achieve that.

You have to have burnt your fingers to know the real danger of fire. You need to have tripped over the banana skin - in public - to realise the embarrassment that comes from not watching where you are going.

You need to lose your way to realise the value of a compass. You need to be let down once or twice, to realise and accept personal disappointment, but not, I hasten to add, to destroy your overall faith in people.

You need to know that what is right today maybe wrong tomorrow and what is wrong today, should sometimes very definitely be tried again tomorrow.

You need to know that being in business is a bit like walking on shifting sands. One moment firm, the next unpredictably slipping away. In selling an idea, don't oversell it ... to yourself!

You need to know how to cut your losses, play the percentage game - golfers will recognise the term - pitch for the heart of a green rather than try to be too clever and, again using a golfing metaphor, get top advice and "read the greens" with a good caddy.

You need to know when to trust your own judgment against someone else's. And, when not to.

You need to be able to set priorities.

Most important of all, you need to be able to read people, to understand what makes them tick, what they are after.

Very little of this is in any book, although to some extent it is what these weekly letters have been about. They are, however, only pieces of paper to be read, and then filed away.

The "street wise" person has it in his bones, in his blood, in every fibre of his being. Whatever he does is instinctive and, quite often, right.

So, who is "street wise"? The person who always seems to have the ball at his feet and to be scoring goals; he also possibly has some gray hairs. How do you become wise? Don't be afraid to make mistakes.

HARNESSING YOUR RESOURCES

In the first of these letters I drew on the game of chess to make the point about gaining the tempo in situations.

I want to draw on it again to make another point - HARNESSING YOUR RESOURCES.

On the chess board, you have a number of pieces, the King, the Queen, two castles, two bishops, two knights, and eight pawns. They all move in different ways and have different functions and they all can contribute to winning the game.

The skill lies in developing them, combining them, and harnessing them. Sending one off on a frolic of its own usually gains nothing. Even the modest pawn, that can never move backwards, has an important part to play, and occasionally can be promoted to be any other piece than the King itself - mutiny is not permitted! I am sure that you can see what I am getting at.

One of this company's greatest strengths lies in the human resources at its disposal. This is reflected in very diverse knowledge and skills. There is also quite a bit of "street wisdom" about. Just look for the grey hairs!

People, however, don't automatically pool their resources, even though everyone is usually better off when they do. Sometimes, they hold something in reserve, they don't like to volunteer, they get on with their job, they are like that legion of waitresses that know the art of not catching your eye. They are never quite there when you want them.

How much are you losing? You are probably the best judge of that because some people have the knack of getting the best out of people, whilst others miss out. Do you take a company view or a narrow branch view? Do you destroy barriers between office staff and sales staff, or do you tolerate them? Do you work with the backroom staff in Villiers Street, or do you just use them?

Do you state what you need or demand what you expect? Do you listen and look, or don't you feel you have to? Do you really fight for your staff, or do you feel there's no great need?

Do you know what "really fighting" means? Not taking "No" for an answer, being prepared to step out of line, putting your head above the parapet, making a nuisance of yourself, but at the end of the day getting things done.

I have long taken the view that if half a dozen people together get behind a project there is nothing they cannot achieve. It does require single-mindedness of purpose and community of interest.

Exercise: Write down the people that you personally can draw on within SCS. 'Then, put a tick besides those that make a sizeable contribution now, and a cross' besides those who could make a sizeable contribution tomorrow' ... or later today!

KAIZEN

I feel quite a sense of achievement to have reached letter number 50 without, I hope, repeating myself too much.

However, as a cautionary reminder to myself as well as to you my theme this week is "KAIZEN".

We are in the middle of a Japanese Festival, Nissan is right on our doorsteps, so it is only right that we should try to draw on the expertise that has made them so successful and so competitive. What does "Kaizen" mean? It means "Continuous improvement"!

One of the great strengths of this company is that we are constantly striving, that we are never satisfied, that we are forever looking at ourselves, at others, defining and refining what we do and, maybe, redefining it as well.

If that is what this company is doing, what are you personally doing?

It is worth giving yourself a few quiet hours - not minutes - to work out your own personal agenda for Kaizen.

It may be little things like letter writing- little but not unimportant. It may be improving man/woman management. You never ever reach the end of that road. It may be product knowledge or appreciating colour and design. I could add to this list, but I am leaving you to do the brainstorming. You might get some ideas by reading again the 49 letters that preceded this one!

You need a written action plan, prioritised, with a timetable, capable of being discussed, progressed and ultimately evaluated. Anything other than that and consign it straight into the dustbin of good intentions!

It is absolutely right to feel a great sense of satisfaction when things go right, but the devil rides pillion all the time tempting you into smug, even arrogant complacency, accepting second best because it might suffice.

Also, what about a bit of Kaizen for those about you? That means encouraging people to look critically at themselves, at each other and at you! And no-one being afraid of facing up to that criticism.

The devil will say that all this is a bit unfair, that it imposes too much pressure, that it really isn't necessary, that you should leave people to set their own standards. In so many establishments that is exactly what he does say, and no-one shows him the door!

The truth is learning never stops, growing never stops, and the fruits of life are there for those who recognise this. Exercise for the week - the month - the year - take this on board and spread the message.

BUSINESS ETHICS

Business ethics - some people, especially those not involved in the world of business and commerce may imagine that these two words just do not go together. They may have a view that business is usually "dirty business." Competition brings out the worst in people!

Well, they could not get it more wrong, I am not going to say that business is pure. I am certainly not going to say that it is noble. What I do say is that it has a built-in code where self- interest happily dovetails with a wider interest.

Business relationships very often are long term. When you have found a supplier or a customer you want to keep him. It can be costly and wasted time to have to replace him. The fact that you are going to make a profit out of your relationship with him does not mean that those relationships cannot be a win-win- win situation.

Marks & Spencer understands this, though they did not do so at first. They had to learn. Initially, they abused relationships. The Japanese certainly understand this and play the long game.

If it is in your interests to play the long game, you just must be straight and above board. You can be a bit mean, but if you are too mean, and it shows, the relationship will break down.

But what about your attitude to your competitor? My father once told me that competitors wouldn't even talk to each other. That's childish. Sometimes it is in your interest to do things together. Sometimes you actually need each other. There must, however, be no illusion in that when it comes to the crunch, he is your competitor and as the old saying goes, if you see a competitor drowning you stick a hosepipe down his throat.

There is no sentimentality here but no hypocrisy either. This is where nature is red in tooth and claw. It is not unethical!

What is happening here is very simple. You go for what you are after with determination to the nth degree. You are under no illusion; he will be doing the same. It really is the only way to succeed. Never mind succeed, it sometimes is the only way to survive.

What about the stress of this? What about the worry? There's an old story of a man who wakes his wife up in the middle of the night. "I just can't get to sleep. I owe Harry a million pounds "Go to sleep" his wife says, "Let him do the worrying." You have got to steel yourself not to worry about the other guy. He isn't going to worry about you!

It's a rough, tough world out there in business, it is no place for weaklings.

Now what about professional ethic? That's slightly different. The lawyer has a duty to his client. He also has a duty to the court. The doctor has a duty to his patient. He also has a wider responsibility. That is why the lawyer cannot himself say something he knows is not true. That is why doctors cannot commit euthanasia. The businessman has some wider obligations but usually they are defined by law.

THE AUTHOR

Alan Share was born in Sunderland in 1933.

He was educated in Bede Grammar School, Sunderland and Merton College, Oxford gaining a degree in Jurisprudence.

Initially he turned his back on his family furniture business opened by his grandfather at the end of the nineteenth century. His chosen career at that time was the Law.

He became a barrister, but he practiced for only three years. He then went to work for the Liberal Party in London becoming the right-hand man of its Secretary at the time, Douglas Robinson. He acted as secretary to the Party Council and Executive and was responsible for the Annual Assembly of the Party.

In the sixties, when his father had cancer, he returned to Sunderland to join his mother Esther run the family retail furnishing business and he opened a new store in the centre of Sunderland's shopping centre. In 1973 friends in the trade told him that furniture retailing was moving out of town and "going discount" and that he need a manager. He recruited Mike Browne, then the manager of a leading furniture retailer in Sunderland. And they opened the *Sunderland Suite Centre* in their original shop selling only upholstered furniture.

This was an immediate success and together with his mother Esther, they grew the company in Northeast England, giving it the name SCS to establish its own identity and its brand. He and his mother both retired in the nineteen nineties, selling the company on a management buy-out to Mike Browne and retaining no financial interest in it thereafter. He was 60 at the time and his mother was over ninety, but still as active as ever!

He was a member of the National Association of Retail Furnishers and became chairman of its Merchandise Committee. He played a lead role in securing the designers of Government's flammability labels when they legislated to require upholstery to be fire-retardant.

He also became a director of the British Shops and Stores Association and in that role, he chaired a nationwide committee that set up the *Qualitas* Conciliation (now known as the Furniture Ombudsman) for the Furniture and Carpet Industry.

He was for many years the chair of the board of *Philip Cussins House*, a residential care home in Newcastle.

More recently he was the chair of TYDFAS, the Newcastle branch of the National Association of Decorative and Fine Arts Societies, now known at the Arts Society.

But in his retirement his membership of the Rotary Club of Sunderland introduced him to the late Fredwyn Haynes, then the head teacher of Barbara *Priestman* School, an all-age school for children with physical disabilities and learning difficulties. When the flavour of the times was to close special schools under the soundbite of Inclusion and the parents, teachers, and the children themselves wanted the school to stay as it was and mounted a campaign to save it, this was to dominate the early years of his retirement. It provoked him to write and stage in London the play *Death of a Nightingale* and publish a book with the same name.

He tells the story in his autobiography *MY ENGLAND,* but he cannot publish it, unable to get the consent of the owners of the copyright of all the images he would like to include.

He has, however, recently published *Death of a Nightingale 2022* with illustrations replacing photographs and with uncomfortable questions for educationalists and lawyers to answer.

He married his wife Ros in 1968, with shared values and enthusiasms and gaining a knowledge of psychology absent from his education.

Together they travelled widely, enjoyed music and the arts and were never, ever bored, Their riches in their family and friends.

If Great Britain had surrendered to Hitler, his life would have ended long ago in a gas chamber along with millions of others. Were it not for the medical profession and the NHS he would not be here today. Were it not for his teachers his life would not have been so rewarding. He sees his writing as an act of Rotary service.

In June 2008 "Featured Author" of the month - Oxford Alumni and Blackwell publishers.

EXTRACT FROM MY ENGLAND

A few of my family and friends are also more equal than others. This picture is very special

In the centre Bill Field, and the baby his first granddaughter. In the Black Watch he escaped from Dunkirk. When he became van driver, his wife asked for more pay and he got it. England at its best.

On the left, Mike Browne who became boss of SCS plc. Esther Share, my mother, worked in her father's office in her teens and in SCS till she was over 90.

Steve Ditch, on the right, shamed me! When he was a skinhead Bill Hardy, warehouse manager told him to wear a cap till his hair grew. When Bill died, Steve told me he visited his widow. A van driver for SCS for over 20 years and a family man.

When *SCS* was a family business

Don't under-value family businesses! Their essence is mutual respect

QUALITAS

Furniture C Carpet Action Committee

An extract from an article.

This story began many years ago when I visited the Danish *Ombudsman* in Copenhagen. It influenced how I organised my own office ever since! He explained to me that he was on the side of the citizen against the State. He didn't sit opposite his client across a table or across a desk. He sat sideways on. Ever since I have always tried to avoid putting a desk or a table between me and the person I was dealing with.

The *Ombudsman* came to the UK in 1967 with great expectations. Now you can find one handling your complaints in Finance, Furniture, Property and more besides.

The *Furniture Ombudsman* has evolved from the conciliation process instituted in an organisation we called *Qualitas*. In 1992 I was the chairman of the Furniture & Carpet Action Committee charged with the task of creating it. We represented the leading carpet and furniture manufacturers and retailers in the UK. Allied Maples, Alston, British Vita, Courts, Stag, MFI, Christie- Tyler, Silentnight, BSSA, BCMA, BFM, Branded Furniture, Retail Consortium and FIRA

It was there to mediate in an even-handed way and, when same complaint repeated itself, to alert those responsible and prevent their recurrence. I have been retired for many years. I wouldn't know how it is working out today.

30 YEARS LATER

Excellent

Rated 4.7 / 5 based on 348934 reviews

poltronesofà ScS

STOP PRESS

£99.4m ScS takeover by Poltronesofa moves forward as shareholders vote in favour

Poltronesofà was established in 1995 and operates 167 furniture and home decor stores in Italy, 106 in France and 27 stores spread across Belgium, Switzerland, Cyprus and Malta.

22 December 2023

LIFE MANAGEMENT SKILLS

A Letter to my 11,518 Connections in Linkedin

"Life Management skills" – Still writing 30 years later!

While I was reading Jurisprudence at Merton, Oxford about 70 years ago – not a typo, I have just turned 90 – I can still recall the late and eminent Professor Herbert Hart's lecture on the word "*Right*". You had to be careful how you used the word, as its meaning changed in use.

But not then, nor since, have I heard anyone say what should happen when human rights clash. They are simply deemed to be equal and absolute. In my long life, more than once they have been different and relative. And they have clashed.

My first book, *Death of a Nightingale with ispy* was a polemic that asserted the rights of children with special needs against the State's steam roller. The children had a right to mainstream education and an equal opportunity to go to university that the Local Education Authority asserted. But here the children and their parents, and over 14,000 putting their names to reasoned objections to closure, preferred their parents' statutory right to the school of their choice, their existing school. Although the Government of the day kept the school open, today it is nothing remotely like the school that it was. The LEA lost the battle but won the war.

Eleven years later, in *Death of a Nightingale 2022*, I am bringing the book up to date. Its publication has been delayed because the Editor of the *Sunderland Echo* has asserted the right of ownership of the copyright to his paper's photographs and prevented me including any of the historic photographs of the parents' campaign. His paper's coverage of the campaign on the front page and double page reports helped the parents to generate the massive protest against closure.

I have commissioned illustrations in their place. The photographs can be found in the *British Library shelfmark MFM.SP385.* My right to free expression in the public interest has lost out.

My new book is a polemic asserting the rights of many more people, in particular the rights of all those children who do not want to go to university with a large debt for life on their back; the ones, like the ones above, who do not want to be educated to fail. They need a different curriculum they can pass with flying colours, with a *5 Star Award* that they can aspire to. Not equal to a degree, different. Theirs. They need an "Opportunity" that doesn't have to be equal, but it should be real. Self-esteem not parity of esteem the purpose.

Today it is no wonder that there are skill shortages to be met by immigration. It is no wonder kids have attention deficit hyperactivity ADHD to be treated with Ritalin. Could it be a tantrum at brain food they do not like? Some kids may need

Ritalin, but multitudinous? No one had this diagnosis in my day.

After the suicide of their daughters, recently the *"Three Dads' Walk"* to the four Parliaments in the UK drew attention to the fact that suicide is the biggest killer of young people across the entire UK.

In yesterday's Times, I read that 8.4 million adults in the UK are prescribed anti-depressant drugs in the UK, and *"one in four adults are prescribed potentially addictive drugs"*. In the headline *"avoid US-style opioid crisis."*

The answer *"The NHS plan recommends that patients be sent to art, music or gardening classes."* All of this would be in an alternative curriculum! And much else besides that would feed curious minds.

My writing goes beyond this.

Today, in the quest for power there are those on the Left and on the Right who want to make the country ungovernable to gain power for themselves. In the USA, it is Trumpism. In the UK it is the Unions representing nurses, doctors, teachers, and railway workers. They assert the right to protest by strike action putting all the blame on the present Government's faults when often they relate to previous ones as well. And with the NHS back to 1948; it is now the victim of its own success.

The right to strike is seen as being *"equal"* and *"absolute."* You cannot question it. Nurses and doctors have the right to strike. But after Covid that is delaying treatment for millions, what about the right of NHS patients to that treatment without unnecessary delay? Teachers have the right to strike. But again, after Covid, pupils have the right to catch up their learning without unnecessary interruption. What about their rights?

Sometimes rights are *"different"* and *"relative"* and you have to assert them, or you lose them altogether. Sometimes freedom of expression loses out badly. Lawyers should put it right urgently.

Wakey, Wakey! Rise and Shine!

MY TELESCOPE

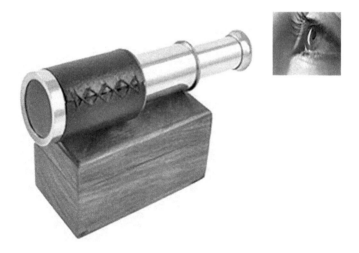

**I do not use my telescope in a
Library. I use my specs there.**
I use it to see people, but not to exploit them.

I see a kaleidoscope of people.

Some to work with or be friends with. Some good, a
few positively evil. Some hungry for power and wealth,
others putting service before self, some wise, and
some foolish. Some good with their brains, some with
their hands, musicians both, some extraordinarily
talented others less so, but none the worse for that.

I use my telescope the right way round.

I see that people are not all equal. And they are not just digits on a computer screen. They are all different. All should have an opportunity to make a success of their lives.

Use a telescope the wrong way round, and that is when people all look the same.

Some hold their telescope to their blind eye!

I am still a Liberal and you can be too, whatever your political allegiance.

POST SCRIPT

Do you know the lyric from Porgy & Bess *"It ain't necessarily so"*? All my life I have been learning from living, working for reward from the age of about thirty to sixty and working for satisfaction from sixty to ninety one. If people tell you that profit is exploitation and the public service is noble, well, *it ain't necessarily so.*

Borough Road Sunderland

When, a teenager, I survived the Blitz in Sunderland in North East England in the 1940's, I chose the Law as my career. It didn't work out. Even after I returned home ten years later for my living - my father had cancer - and thirty years after that when I retired in 1993, sold it, I could not imagine that a small side-street family furniture shop and still bearing the name of my grandfather, could morph into a company that has just been bought by an Italian company, Poltronesofà, for £99m; I have had no part of it since then, but I had helped it on its way.

It was a win for the company and those who worked in it, a win for those who owned it, a win for those who supplied it and, with Trustpilot recording 348,934 reviews for Excellence, a win for its customers. Profit was the measure of its success and the means of securing it. In one word, Capitalism.

Meanwhile, in the last thirty years I could fill this page with the dirty tricks I have witnessed perpetrated in the public service, compounded by lawyers and civil servants. Often they asserted the human rights of some, but totally ignored the rights of others.

Doctors and nurses strike, but patients have their rights too, waiting for treatment and having still longer to wait for it. Teachers strike, but their pupils have a right to their education to pass their exams. Rail-workers strike, but people have a right to get to their work on time. Copyright is asserted against the right to free expression of photographs of events for historical record. &c.

Sometimes politics get in the way of human rights. Sometimes rights clash. Whenever they do, unresolved it is a precursor to anarchy, as everyone asserts their own.

Far too many people believe that what is right for them is right for everyone else as well, when it isn't. The dirty tricks the evidence of their failures.

Meanwhile generations of students study Roman Law.

Very simply power corrupts, first in the quest to gain it, then in the quest to keep it. Money can corrupt too when it is power. And lawyers sometimes provide the tools for the job.

The challenge in a democratic society – and the difference from a dictatorship - is to make those with power accountable for their use of it, and efficient. All the way to go. So much today is a charade, and afterwards comes the inevitable disappointment.

A CHALLENGE

*Equal only sometimes, unequal most times,
always different*

*POLITICIANS

*TEACHERS

*LAWYERS

Read Death of a Nightingale 2024 NEW EDITION and discuss.

Available on Amazon soon.
For more information you can visit
www.deathofanightingale.com

Milton Keynes UK
Ingram Content Group UK Ltd.
UKHW021855260524
443211UK00001BA/68

9 781963 883732